Practical Automated
Machine Learning on Azure

*Using Azure Machine Learning
to Quickly Build AI Solutions*

*Deepak Mukunthu, Parashar Shah,
and Wee Hyong Tok*

Beijing · Boston · Farnham · Sebastopol · Tokyo

Practical Automated Machine Learning on Azure

by Deepak Mukunthu, Parashar Shah, and Wee Hyong Tok

Published by O'Reilly Media, Inc., 1005 Gravenstein Highway North, Sebastopol, CA 95472.

O'Reilly books may be purchased for educational, business, or sales promotional use. Online editions are also available for most titles (*http://oreilly.com*). For more information, contact our corporate/institutional sales department: 800-998-9938 or *corporate@oreilly.com*.

Acquisitions Editor: Jonathan Hassell	**Indexer:** Judith McConville
Development Editor: Nicole Tache	**Interior Designer:** David Futato
Production Editor: Deborah Baker	**Cover Designer:** Karen Montgomery
Copyeditor: Octal Publishing, LLC	**Illustrator:** Rebecca Demarest
Proofreader: Sharon Wilkey	

September 2019:   First Edition

Revision History for the First Edition
2019-09-20:   First Release

See *http://oreilly.com/catalog/errata.csp?isbn=9781492055594* for release details.

The O'Reilly logo is a registered trademark of O'Reilly Media, Inc. *Practical Automated Machine Learning on Azure*, the cover image, and related trade dress are trademarks of O'Reilly Media, Inc.

978-1-492-05559-4

[LSI]

Dedicated to my wife, kids, and parents for their unconditional love, encouragement and support in everything I do.
—Deepak

Dedicated to the wonderful individuals in my life—Juliet, Nathaniel, and Jayden. My gratitude and love for them is infinite.
—Wee Hyong

I would like to thank my parents Nita and Mahendra and my sister Vidhi for their unconditional love and encouragement throughout my life. I am thankful to my buddies at Microsoft—Priya, Premal, Vicky, Martha, Savita, Deepti, and Sagar—and my buddies outside of Microsoft—Kevin, Ritu, Dhaval, Shamit, Priyadarshan, Pradip, and Nikhil—for their loving friendship.
—Parashar

Table of Contents

Part II.   Automated ML on Azure

Foreword

I vividly remember my first undergraduate class in artificial intelligence (AI). My father had worked for years on "expert systems," and I was at MIT to learn from the best how to perform this wizardry. Marvin Minsky, one of the founders of the field, even taught a series of guest lectures there. It was about midway through the semester when the great disillusionment hit me: "It's all just a bunch of tricks!" There was no "intelligence" to be found; just a bunch of brittle rules engines and clever use of math. This was in the early '90s and the start of my own personal AI winter, when I dismissed AI as not having much use.

Years later, while I was working on advertising systems, I finally saw that there was power in this "bunch of tricks." Algorithms that had been hand-tuned for months by talented engineers were being beaten by simple models provided with lots of data. I saw that the explosion that was to come simply needed more data and more computation to be effective. Over the past 5 to 10 years, the explosion in both big data and computation power has unleashed an industry that has had lots of starts and stops to it.

This time is different. While the hype about AI is still tremendously high, the potential applications of practical AI have really just begun to hit the business world. The rules or people making predictions today will be replaced virtually every place by AI algorithms. The value AI creates for businesses is tremendous, from being better able to value the oil available in an oil field to better predicting the inventory a store should stock of each new sneaker. Even marginal improvements in these capabilities represent billions of dollars of value across businesses.

We're now in an age of AI implementation. Companies are working to find all the best places to deploy AI in their enterprises. One of the biggest challenges is matching the hype to reality. Half the companies I've talked to expect AI to perform some kind of magic for problems they have no idea how to solve. The other half are underestimating the power that AI can have. What they need are people with enough background in AI to help them conceive of what is possible and apply it to their business problems.

Customers I talk to are struggling to find enough people with those skills. While they have lots of developers and data analysts who are skilled and comfortable making predictions and decisions with data, they need data scientists who can then build the model from that data. This book will help fill that gap.

It shows how automated ML can empower developers and data analysts to train AI models. It highlights a number of business cases where AI is a great fit to the business problem and show exactly how to build that model and put it into production. The technology and ideas in this book have been pressure-tested at scale with teams all across Microsoft, including Bing, Office, Azure Security, internal IT, and many more. It's also been used by many external businesses using Azure Machine Learning.

— Eric Boyd
Microsoft Corporate Vice President, Azure AI
September 2019

Preface

Conventions Used in This Book

The following typographical conventions are used in this book:

Italic
> Indicates new terms, URLs, email addresses, filenames, and file extensions.

`Constant width`
> Used for program listings, as well as within paragraphs to refer to program elements such as variable or function names, databases, data types, environment variables, statements, and keywords.

`Constant width bold`
> Shows commands or other text that should be typed literally by the user.

`Constant width italic`
> Shows text that should be replaced with user-supplied values or by values determined by context.

 This element signifies a tip or suggestion.

 This element signifies a general note.

This element indicates a warning or caution.

Using Code Examples

Supplemental material (code examples, exercises, etc.) is available for download at *https://oreil.ly/Practical_Automated_ML_on_Azure*.

This book is here to help you get your job done. In general, if example code is offered with this book, you may use it in your programs and documentation. You do not need to contact us for permission unless you're reproducing a significant portion of the code. For example, writing a program that uses several chunks of code from this book does not require permission. Selling or distributing a CD-ROM of examples from O'Reilly books does require permission. Answering a question by citing this book and quoting example code does not require permission. Incorporating a significant amount of example code from this book into your product's documentation does require permission.

We appreciate, but do not require, attribution. An attribution usually includes the title, author, publisher, and ISBN. For example: "*Practical Automated Machine Learning on Azure* by Deepak Mukunthu, Parashar Shah, and Wee Hyong Tok (O'Reilly). Copyright 2019 Deepak Mukunthu, Parashar Shah, and Wee Hyong Tok, 978-1-492-05559-4."

If you feel your use of code examples falls outside fair use or the permission given above, feel free to contact us at *permissions@oreilly.com*.

O'Reilly Online Learning

 For almost 40 years, *O'Reilly Media* has provided technology and business training, knowledge, and insight to help companies succeed.

Our unique network of experts and innovators share their knowledge and expertise through books, articles, conferences, and our online learning platform. O'Reilly's online learning platform gives you on-demand access to live training courses, in-depth learning paths, interactive coding environments, and a vast collection of text and video from O'Reilly and 200+ other publishers. For more information, please visit *http://oreilly.com*.

How to Contact Us

Please address comments and questions concerning this book to the publisher:

O'Reilly Media, Inc.
1005 Gravenstein Highway North
Sebastopol, CA 95472
800-998-9938 (in the United States or Canada)
707-829-0515 (international or local)
707-829-0104 (fax)

The web page for this book lists errata, examples, and additional information. You can access this page at *http://www.oreilly.com/catalog/9781492055594*.

To comment or ask technical questions about this book, send email to *bookquestions@oreilly.com*.

For more information about our books, courses, conferences, and news, see our website at *http://www.oreilly.com*.

Find us on Facebook: *http://facebook.com/oreilly*

Follow us on Twitter: *http://twitter.com/oreillymedia*

Watch us on YouTube: *http://www.youtube.com/oreillymedia*

Acknowledgments

This book wouldn't have been possible without great contributions from these folks–*thank you!*

We are thankful to our coworkers at Microsoft (Azure AI product, marketing, and many other teams) for working together to deliver the best enterprise-ready Azure Machine Learning service.

Nicolo Fusi, for sharing details on research that lead to the creation of Automated ML (Chapter 2).

Sharon Gillett, for text inputs to Automated ML introduction (Chapter 2).

Vanessa Milan, for images for Automated ML introduction (Chapter 2).

Akchara Mukunthu, for example scenarios for Machine Learning task detection (Table 2-1 in Chapter 2).

Krishna Anumalasetty and Thomas Abraham, for technical review of the book.

Jen Stirrup, for feedback on the book.

The amazing O'Reilly team (Nicole Tache, Deborah Baker, Bob Russell, Jonathan Hassell, Ben Lorica, and many more), for working with us from concept to production and giving us the opportunity to write and share the book with the community.

Members of the Azure Machine Learning and Azure CAT team, for the supportive environment that enabled the authors to write the book during their off hours, and many weekends and holidays.

## PART I

Automated Machine Learning

In this part, you will learn how Automated Machine Learning can help automate model development.

## CHAPTER 1

Machine Learning: Overview and Best Practices

How are humans different from machines? There are quite a few differences, but here's an important one: humans learn from experience, whereas machines follow instructions given to them. What if machines can also learn from experience? That is the crux of machine learning. For machines, "data from the past" is the logical equivalent of "experience." Machine learning combines statistics and computer science to enable machines to learn how to perform a given task without being explicitly programmed to do so via instructions.

Machine learning is widely used today, and we interact with it every day. Here are a few examples to illu strate:

- Search engines like Bing or Google
- Product recommendations at online stores like Amazon or eBay
- Personalized video recommendations at Netflix or YouTube
- Voice-based digital assistants like Alexa or Cortana
- Spam filters for our email inbox
- Credit card fraud detection

Why is machine learning as a trend emerging so fast? Why is everyone so interested in it *now*? As shown in Figure 1-1, its popularity arises from three key trends: big data, better/cheaper compute, and smarter algorithms.

Machine Learning–Why Now?		
Bigger Data	**Better Hardware**	**Smarter Algorithms**
Flood of digital information that doubles every three years	Optimized chips improving faster than Moore's law Cheap storage and bandwidth	Ability to handle real-world complexity Training time down ~80% since 2010

Figure 1-1. Machine learning growth

In this chapter, we provide a quick refresher on machine learning by using a real-world example, discuss some of the best practices that differentiate successful machine learning projects from the rest, and end with challenges around productivity and scale.

Machine Learning: A Quick Refresher

What does the process of building a machine learning model look like? Let's dig deeper using a real scenario: house price prediction. We have past home sales data, and the task is to predict the sale price for a given house that just came onto the market and isn't currently in our dataset.

For simplicity, let's assume that the size of the house (in square feet) is the most important input attribute (or *feature*) that determines house value. As shown in Table 1-1, we have data from four houses, A, B, C, D, and we need to predict the price of house X.

Table 1-1. House prices based on size

House	Size (sq. ft)	Price ($)
A	1300	500,000
B	2000	800,000
C	2500	950,000
D	3200	1,200,000
X	1800	?

We begin by plotting *Size* on the x-axis and *Price* on the y-axis, as shown in Figure 1-2.

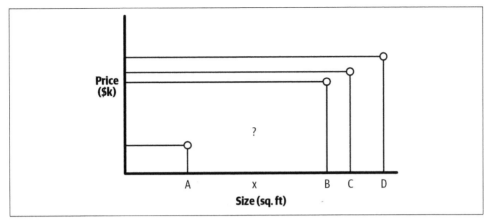

Figure 1-2. Plotting price versus size

What's the best estimate for the price of house X?

- $550,000
- $700,000
- $1,000,000

Let's figure it out. As shown in Figure 1-3, the four points that we plotted based on the data form an almost straight line. If we draw this line that best fits our data, we can find the right point on the line associated with house X on the x-axis and the corresponding point on y-axis, which will give us our price estimate.

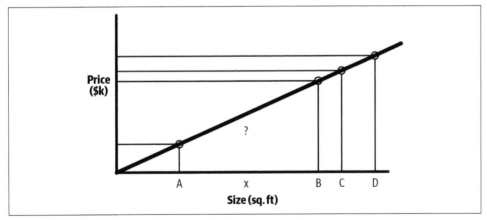

Figure 1-3. Creating a straight line to find price estimate

In this case, that straight line represents our model—and demonstrates a linear relationship. *Linear regression* is a statistical approach for modeling a linear relationship between *input variables* (also called *feature*, or *independent*, *variables*) and an *output variable* (also called a *target*, or *dependent*, *variable*). Mathematically, this linear relationship can be represented as follows:

$$y = \beta 0 + \beta 1 x$$

where:

- y is the output variable; for example, the house price.
- x is the input variable; for example, size in square feet.
- $\beta 0$ is the intercept (the value of y when $x = 0$).
- $\beta 1$ is the coefficient for x and the slope of the regression line ("the average increase in y associated with a one-unit increase in x).

Model Parameters

$\beta 0$ and $\beta 1$ are known as the *model parameters* of this linear regression model. When implementing linear regression, the algorithm finds the line of best fit by using the model parameters $\beta 0$ and $\beta 1$, such that it is as close as possible to the actual data points (minimizing the sum of the squared distances between each actual data point and the line representing model predictions).

Figure 1-4 shows this conceptually. Dots represent actual data points, and the line represents the model predictions. *d1* to *d9* represent distances between data points and the corresponding model prediction, and *D* is the sum of their squares. The line shown in the figure is the best-fit regression line that minimizes *D*.

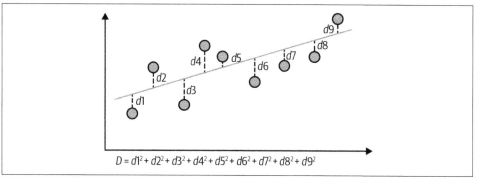

$$D = d1^2 + d2^2 + d3^2 + d4^2 + d5^2 + d6^2 + d7^2 + d8^2 + d9^2$$

Figure 1-4. Regression

As you can see, *model parameters* are an integral part of the model and determine the outcome. Their values are learned from data through the model training process.

Hyperparameters

There is another set of parameters known as *hyperparameters*. Model hyperparameters are used during the *model training process* to establish the correct values of model parameters. They are external to the model, and their values cannot be estimated from data. The choice of the hyperparameters will affect the duration of the training and the accuracy of the predictions. As part of the model training process, data scientists usually specify hyperparameters based on heuristics or knowledge, and often tune the hyperparameters manually. Hyperparameter tuning relies more on experimental results than theory, and thus the best method to determine the optimal settings is to try many combinations and evaluate the performance of each model.

Simple linear regression doesn't have any hyperparameters. But variants of linear regression, like Ridge regression and Lasso (*http://bit.ly/lasso-proj*), do. Here are some examples of model hyperparameters for various machine learning algorithms:

- The k in k-nearest neighbors
- The desired depth and number of leaves in a decision tree
- The C and sigma in support vector machines (SVMs)
- The learning rate for a neural network training

Best Practices for Machine Learning Projects

In this section, we examine best practices that make machine learning projects successful. These are practical tips that most companies and teams end up learning with experience.

Understand the Decision Process

Machine learning–based systems or processes use data to drive business decisions. Hence, it is important to understand the business problem that needs to be solved, independent of technology solutions—in other words, what decision or action needs to be taken that can be informed by data. Being clear about the decision process is critical. This step is also sometimes referred to as *mapping a business scenario/problem to a data science question.*

For our house-price prediction scenario, the key business decision for a home buyer, is "Should I buy a given house at the listed price?" or "What is a good bid price for this house to maximize my chance of winning the bid?" This could be mapped to the data science question: "What is the best estimate of the house price based on past sales data of other houses?"

Table 1-2 shows other real-world business scenarios and what this decision process looks like.

Table 1-2. Understanding a decision process: real-world scenarios

Business scenario	Key decision	Data science question
Predictive maintenance	Should I service this piece of equipment?	What is the probability this equipment will fail within the next x days?
Energy forecasting	Should I buy or sell energy contracts?	What will be the long-/short-term demand for energy in a region?
Customer churn	Which customers should I prioritize to reduce churn?	What is the probability of churn within x days for each customer?
Personalized marketing	What product should I offer first?	What is the probability that customers will purchase each product?
Product feedback	Which service/product needs attention?	What is the social media sentiment for each service/product?

Establish Performance Metrics

As with any project, performance metrics are important to guide any machine learning project toward the proper goals and to ensure progress is made. After we understand the decision process, the next step is to answer these two key questions:

- How do we measure progress toward a goal or desired outcome? In other words, how do we define metrics to evaluate progress?

- What would be considered a success? That is, how do we define targets for the metrics defined?

For our house-price prediction example, we need a metric to measure how close our predictions are to the actual price. There are quite a few metrics to choose from. One of the most commonly used metrics for regression tasks is *root-mean-square error* (RMSE). This is defined as the square root of the average squared distance between the actual score and the predicted score, as shown here:

$$\text{RMSE} = \sqrt{\frac{1}{n}\sum_{j=1}^{n}\left(y_j - \hat{y}_j\right)^2}$$

Here, y_j denotes the true value for the ith data point, and $\hat{y}_j$ denotes the predicted value. One intuitive way to understand this formula is that it is the Euclidean distance between the vector of the true values and the vector of the predicted values, averaged by n, where n is the number of data points.

Focus on Transparency to Gain Trust

There is a common perception that machine learning is a black box that just works magically. It is critical to understand that although model performance as measured by metrics is important, it is even more important for us to understand how the model works. Without this understanding, it is difficult to trust the model and therefore difficult to convince key stakeholders and customers of the business value of machine learning and machine learning–based systems.

In heavily regulated industries like health care and banking, which are required to comply with regulation, interpretability of models is critical. *Model interpretability* is typically represented by feature importance, which tells you how each input column (or feature) affects the model's predictions. This allows data scientists to explain resulting predictions so that stakeholders can see which data points are most important in the model.

In our house-price prediction scenario, our trust on the model would increase if the model, in addition to price prediction, indicated key input features that contributed to the output; for example, house size and age. Figure 1-5 shows feature importance for our house-price prediction scenario. Notice that age and school rating are the top-most features.

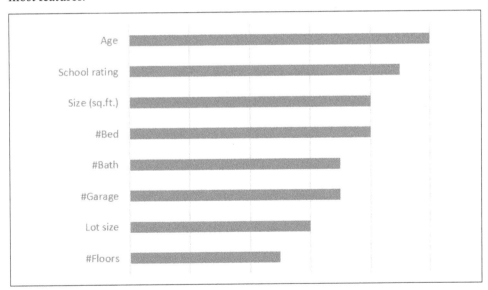

Figure 1-5. Feature importance

Embrace Experimentation

Building a good machine learning model takes time. As with other software projects, the trick to becoming successful in machine learning projects lies in how fast we try out new hypotheses, learn from them, and keep evolving. As shown in Figure 1-6, the path to success isn't usually easy and requires a lot of persistence, due diligence, and failures on the way.

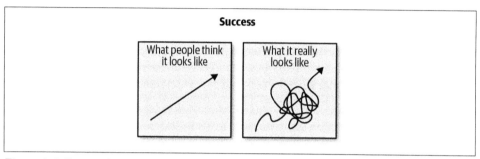

Figure 1-6. Success is not easy.

Here are key aspects of a culture that values experimentation:

- Be willing to learn from experiments (successes or failures).
- Share the learning with peers.
- Promote successful experiments to production.
- Understand that failure is a valid outcome of an experiment.
- Quickly move on to the next hypothesis.
- Refine the next experiment.

Don't Operate in a Silo

Customers typically experience machine learning models through applications. Figure 1-7 shows how machine learning systems are different from traditional software systems. The key difference is that machine learning systems, in addition to code workflow, must also consider data workflow.

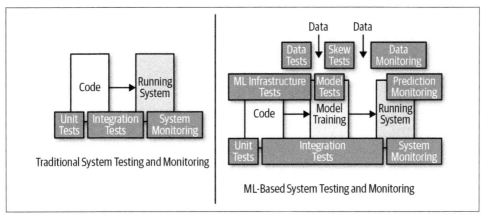

Figure 1-7. Machine learning system versus traditional systems

After data scientists have built a machine learning model that is satisfactory to them, they hand it off to an app developer who integrates it into the larger application and deploys it. Often, any bugs or performance issues go undiscovered until the application has already been deployed. The resulting friction between app developers and data scientists to identify and fix the root cause can be a slow, frustrating, and expensive process.

As machine learning enters more business-critical applications, it is increasingly clear that data scientists need to collaborate closely with app developers to build and deploy machine learning–powered applications more efficiently. Data scientists are focused on the data science life cycle; namely, data ingestion and preparation, model building, and deployment. They are also interested in periodically retraining and redeploying the model to adjust for freshly labeled data, data drift, user feedback, or changes in model inputs. The app developer is focused on the application life cycle— building, maintaining, and continuously updating the larger business application that the model is part of. Both parties are motivated to make the business application and model work well together to meet end-to-end performance, quality, and reliability goals.

What is needed is a way to bridge the data science and application life cycles more effectively. Figure 1-8 shows how this collaboration could be enabled. We will cover this in more depth later in the book.

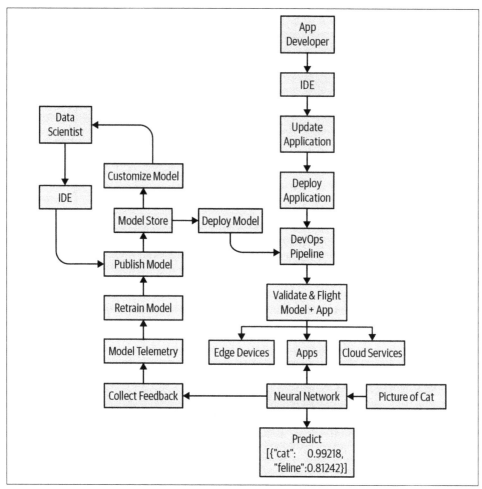

Figure 1-8. App developer and data scientist working together

An Iterative and Time-Consuming Process

In this section, we dig deeper into the machine learning process by using our house-price prediction example. We started with house size as the only input, and we saw the relationship between house size and house price to be linear. To create a good model that can predict prices more accurately, we need to explore good input features, select the best algorithm, and tune hyperparameter values. But, how do you know which features are good, and which algorithm and hyperparameter values will do the best? There is no silver bullet here; we will need to try out different combinations of features, algorithms, and hyperparameter values. Let's take a look at each of these three steps and then see how they apply to our house-price prediction problem.

Feature Engineering

Feature engineering is the process of using our knowledge of the data to create features that make machine learning algorithms work. As shown in Figure 1-9, this involves four steps.

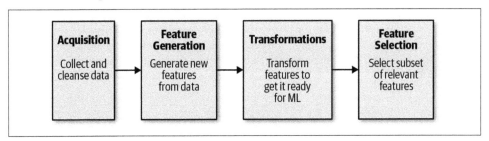

Figure 1-9. Feature engineering

First, we *acquire data*—collect the data with all of these possible input variables/features and get it to a usable state. Most real-world datasets are not clean, and need work to get the data to a level of quality before using it. This can involve things such as fixing missing values, removing anomalies and possibly incorrect data, and ensuring the data distribution is representative.

Next you'll need to *generate features*: explore generating more features from available data. This is typically useful when dealing with text data or time-series data. Text-related features could be as simple as *n*-grams and count vectorization or as advanced as sentiment from review text. Similarly, time-related features could be as simple as month and week-index-of-year or as complex as time-based aggregations. These additional features generated can prove helpful in improving accuracy of the model.

With this complete, you'll need to *transform the data* to make it suitable for machine learning. Often, machine learning algorithms require that data be prepared in specific ways before fitting a machine learning model. For instance, many such algorithms cannot operate on categorical data directly, and require all input variables and output variables be numeric. A *categorical variable* is a variable (*https://oreil.ly/4YTwv*) that can take on one of a limited, and usually fixed, number of possible values. Examples of these variables include color (red, blue, green, etc.), country (United States, India, China, etc.), and blood group (A, B, O, AB). Categorical variables must be converted to a numerical form, which is typically done by using integer encoding or one-hot encoding techniques.

The final step is *feature selection*: choosing a subset of features to train the model on. Why is this necessary? Why not train the model with the full set of features? Feature selection identifies and removes the unneeded, irrelevant, and redundant attributes from data that don't contribute, or can in fact decrease, the model's accuracy. The objective of feature selection is threefold:

- Improve model accuracy

- Improve model training time/cost

- Provide a better understanding of the underlying process of feature generation

 Feature engineering steps are critical for traditional machine learning but not so much for deep learning, because features are automatically generated/inferred through the deep learning network.

We began with a single feature: house size. But we know that the price of a house is dependent not only on size, but also on other characteristics. What other input features could influence *house price*? Although size might be one of the most important inputs, here are few more worth considering:

- Zip code

- Year built

- Lot size

- Schools

- Number of bedrooms

- Number of bathrooms

- Number of garage stalls

- Amenities

Algorithm Selection

After we have chosen a good set of features, the next step is to determine the correct algorithm for the model. For the data we have, a simple linear regression model might seem to work. But remember that we have only a few data points (four houses with price)—small enough to be representative and small enough for machine learning. Also, linear regression assumes a linear relation between input features and target variable. As we collect more data points, linear regression might not remain most relevant, and we will be motivated to explore other techniques (algorithms) depending on trends and patterns in data.

Hyperparameter Tuning

As discussed earlier in this chapter, hyperparameters play a key role in model accuracy and training performance. Hence, tuning them is a critical step in getting to a good model. Because different algorithms have different sets of hyperparameters, this step of tuning hyperparameters adds to the complexity of the end-to-end process.

The End-to-End Process

With that basic understanding of feature engineering, algorithm selection, and hyperparameter tuning, let's go step by step through our house-price prediction problem.

Let's begin with *Size*, *Lot size*, and *Year built* features and *Gradient Boosted* trees with specific hyperparameter values, as shown in Figure 1-10. The resulting model is 30% accurate. But we want to do better than that.

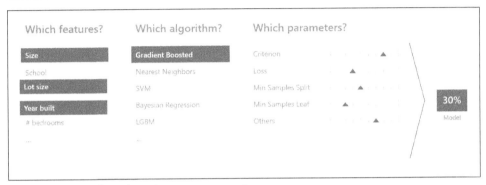

Figure 1-10. Machine learning process: step 1

To get underway, we try different values of hyperparameters for the same set of features and algorithm. If that doesn't improve accuracy of the model to a satisfactory level, we try different algorithms, and if that doesn't help either, we add more features. Figure 1-11 shows one such intermediate state, with School added as a feature and the *k*-nearest neighbors (KNN) algorithm used. The resulting model is 50% accurate but still not good enough, so we continue this process and try different combinations.

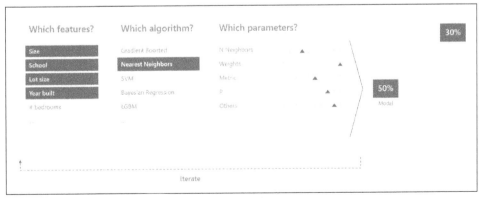

Figure 1-11. Machine learning process: intermediate state

After multiple iterations of trying out different combinations of features, algorithms, and hyperparameter values, we end up with a model that meets our criteria, as shown in Figure 1-12.

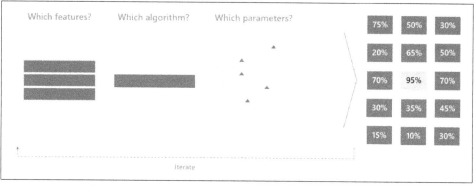

Figure 1-12. Machine learning process: best model

As you can see, this is an iterative and time-consuming process. To put this in perspective: if there are 10 features, there are a total of 2^{10} (1,024) ways to select features. If we try five algorithms, and assuming each has an average of five hyperparameters, we are looking at a total of $1,024 \times 5 \times 5 = 25,600$ iterations!

Figure 1-13 shows the `scikit-learn` cheat sheet demonstrating that choosing the proper algorithm could be a complex problem in itself. Now imagine adding feature engineering and hyperparameter tuning on top of it. As a result, it takes data scientists anywhere from a couple of weeks to months to arrive at a good model.

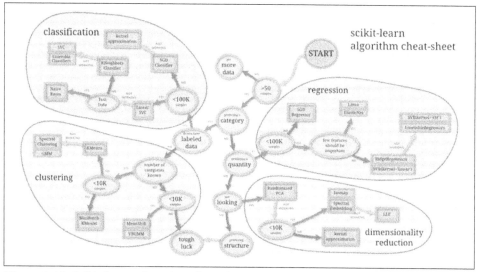

Figure 1-13. Scikit-learn algorithm cheat sheet (source: https://oreil.ly/xUZbU)

Growing Demand

Despite the complexity of the model-building process, demand for machine learning has skyrocketed. Most organizations across all industries are trying to use data and machine learning to gain a competitive advantage—infusing intelligence into their products and processes to delight customers and amplify business impact. Figure 1-14 shows the variety of real-world business problems being solved using machine learning.

```
              Real-World Business Problems

  Improving visibility and making      Getting the right products
      accurate predictions                 to the right places
  - Remote monitoring                   - Inventory management
  - Demand forecasting                  - Supply chain optimization
  - Risk and compliance management      - Marketing mix optimization

  Offering customers exactly what      Fixing problems proactively
     they want, when they want it            before they start
  - Personalized offers                 - Predictive maintenance
  - Product recommendations             - Operational effiency
  - New product introduction            - Customer service improvement

                 Exploring new business
                     opportunities
                - Cross-sell and upsell
                - Product-as-a-service
                - New data-driven services
```

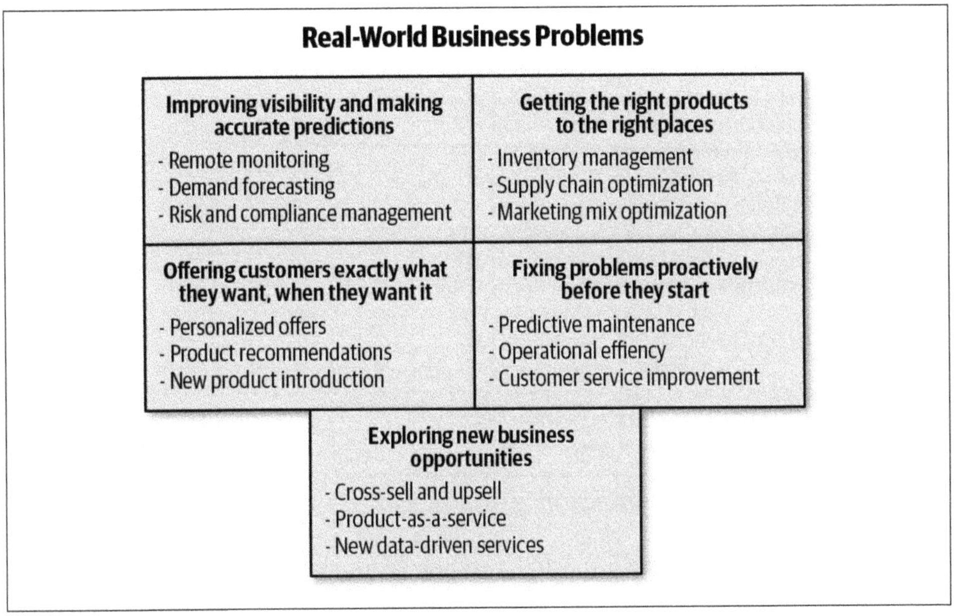

Figure 1-14. Real-world business problems using machine learning

As a result, there is huge demand for machine learning–related jobs. Figure 1-15 shows the percentage growth in various job postings from 2015 to 2018.

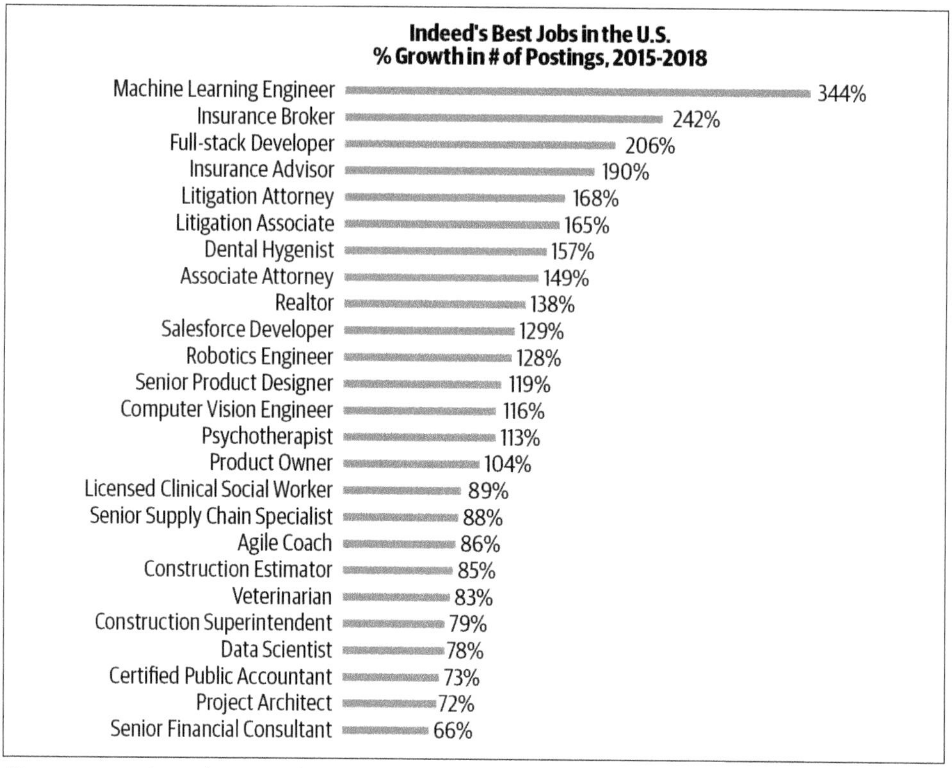

Indeed's Best Jobs in the U.S.
% Growth in # of Postings, 2015-2018

Machine Learning Engineer	344%
Insurance Broker	242%
Full-stack Developer	206%
Insurance Advisor	190%
Litigation Attorney	168%
Litigation Associate	165%
Dental Hygenist	157%
Associate Attorney	149%
Realtor	138%
Salesforce Developer	129%
Robotics Engineer	128%
Senior Product Designer	119%
Computer Vision Engineer	116%
Psychotherapist	113%
Product Owner	104%
Licensed Clinical Social Worker	89%
Senior Supply Chain Specialist	88%
Agile Coach	86%
Construction Estimator	85%
Veterinarian	83%
Construction Superintendent	79%
Data Scientist	78%
Certified Public Accountant	73%
Project Architect	72%
Senior Financial Consultant	66%

Figure 1-15. Growth in machine learning–related jobs

And Figure 1-16 shows the expected revenue from enterprise applications using machine learning and artificial intelligence growing astronomically.

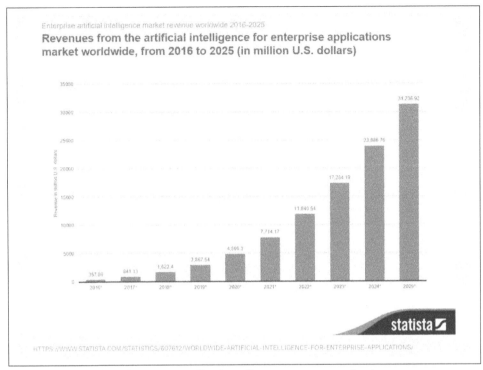

Figure 1-16. Machine learning/artificial intelligence revenue projections

Conclusion

In this chapter, you learned some of the best practices that successful machine learning projects have in common. We discussed that the process of building a good machine learning model is iterative and time-consuming, resulting in data scientists requiring anywhere from a couple of weeks to months to build a good model. At the same time, demand for machine learning is growing rapidly and is expected to sky-rocket.

To balance this supply-versus-demand problem, there needs to be a better way to shorten the time it takes to build machine learning models. Can some of the steps in that workflow be automated? Absolutely! Automated Machine Learning is one of the most important skills that successful data scientists need to have in their toolbox for improved productivity.

In the following chapters we'll go deeper into Automated Machine Learning. We will explore what it is, how to get started, and how it is being used in real-world applications today.

## CHAPTER 2

How Automated Machine Learning Works

In the previous chapter, we established the need to automate the process of building machine learning models. In this chapter, we explain what *Automated Machine Learning* is, the different techniques involved in this process, and how they all come together. We will also give a quick overview of automated ML on Microsoft Azure Machine Learning.

What Is Automated Machine Learning?

In Chapter 1, we discussed how coming up with a good machine learning model can be time-consuming and tedious, given all the possible combinations to explore. Automated Machine Learning is a recent development in machine learning focused on making that entire process easy, with the goal of bringing efficiency to data scientists as well as enabling non–data scientists to build models.

Let's go through the stages of the machine learning process and see how Automated Machine Learning can help at each stage.

Understanding Data

As briefly discussed in the previous chapter, real-world data is not clean and requires a lot of effort to get to a usable state. Understanding input data is a crucial step toward formulating the machine learning problem.

Automated Machine Learning can help here by analyzing the data and automatically detecting the data type of each column. Column types could be Boolean, numeric (discrete or continuous), or text. Automatically detecting these column types helps with subsequent stages like feature engineering.

In many cases, Automated Machine Learning can also provide insight into the semantics or intent of each column. It can detect a wide spectrum of situations, including the following:

- Detecting the target/label column
- Detecting whether a text column is a categorical-text feature or free-text feature
- Detecting columns that are zip codes, temperatures, geo coordinates, and so on

Before we go ahead, let's discuss how the model training process works in relationship to input data. Should we train using all of the data available? The answer is no.

Training the model on the full input data can lead to *overfitting*. Overfitting means that the model we trained is fit too closely to the input dataset and mimics the input dataset. This usually happens when the model is too complex (i.e., too many features/variables compared to the number of observations). This model will be very accurate on the input data but will probably perform badly on untrained or new data.

In contrast, when a model is *underfit*, it means that the model does not fit the input data and therefore misses the trends in the data. It also means the model cannot be generalized to new data. This is usually the result of a very simple model (not enough input variables/features). Adding more input variables/features helps overcome underfitting.

Figure 2-1 shows overfitting and underfitting for a binary classification problem.

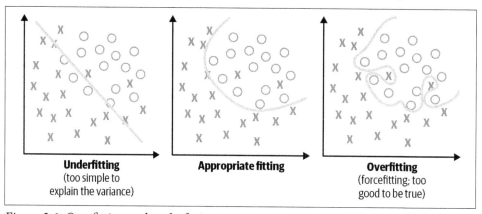

Figure 2-1. Overfitting and underfitting

To overcome the overfitting problem, we usually split input data into two subsets: training data and testing data (and sometimes further, into three subsets: train, validate, and test). The model is then fit on the training data to make predictions on the test data. The training set contains a known output, and the model learns on this so that it can generalize to other data later. We use the test set to test the accuracy of our model's predictions.

But, how do we know if the train/test split is good? What if one subset of our data is skewed compared to the other? This will result in overfitting, even though we're trying to avoid that. This is where cross-validation comes in.

Cross-validation is similar to the train/test split, but it's applied to more subsets. Data is split into k subsets, and the model is trained on $k - 1$ of those subsets. The last subset is held for testing. This is done for each of the subsets. This is called k-fold cross-validation. Finally, the scores from all the k-folds are averaged to produce the final score. Figure 2-2 shows this.

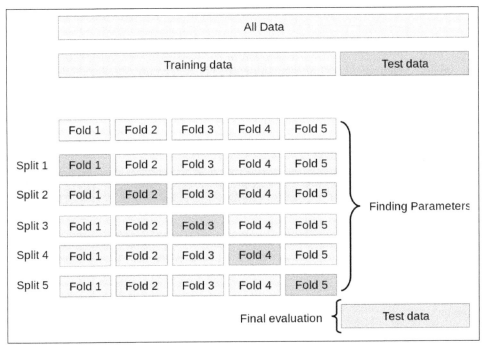

Figure 2-2. k-fold cross-validation (source: ttps://oreil.ly/k-ixI)

Detecting Tasks

Data scientists map real-world scenarios to machine learning tasks. Figure 2-3 shows some examples of types of machine learning tasks.

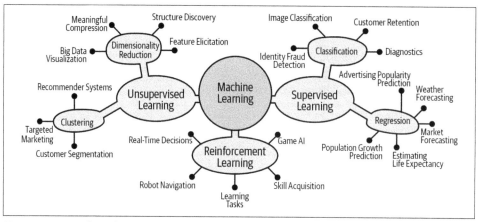

Figure 2-3. Machine learning tasks

Automated Machine Learning can automatically determine the machine learning task, given the input data. This is more relevant in *supervised machine learning*, in which target/label columns can be used to predict the machine learning task. Table 2-1 lists generic machine learning tasks.

Table 2-1. Machine learning task detection

Target/Label column	Machine learning task	Example scenarios
Boolean	Binary classification	* Classifying sentiment of Twitter comments (*https://oreil.ly/baZaJ*) as either positive or negative * Indicating that email is spam or not
Discrete numerical/ categorical	Multiclass classification	* Determining the breed of a dog as Havanese, Golden Retriever, Beagle, etc. * Categorizing hotel reviews by location, price, cleanliness, etc.
Continuous numerical	Regression	* Predicting house prices based on house attributes such as number of bedrooms, location, or size * Predicting future stock prices based on historical data and current market trends

In addition to these generic tasks, there are specific variations based on input data. Forecasting is one such task type that is popular, given its relevance to many business problems like revenue forecasting, inventory management, predictive maintenance, and so on. If input data is time-series, determined by availability of a DateTime column, it is most likely a forecasting task.

Choosing Evaluation Metrics

Choosing a metric to evaluate your machine learning algorithm is fundamentally driven by the business outcome. This is an important step because it tells you how the performance of your algorithm is measured and compared. Different tasks have different sets of evaluation metrics to choose from, and the choice depends on multiple factors. Figure 2-4 shows possible options for evaluating algorithms used in various machine learning tasks.

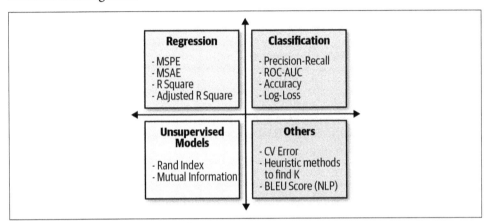

Figure 2-4. Machine learning evaluation metrics

Automated Machine Learning can automate the process of selecting the right evaluation metric for a given input dataset and machine learning task. For instance, scenarios like fraud detection (which is a classification task) inherently have imbalanced data in that a very small percentage of data would be fraudulent. In this case, area under curve (AUC) is a much better evaluation metric than accuracy. Automatically detecting class imbalance in the data can help automatically choose AUC as an evaluation metric for this classification task.

Feature Engineering

As discussed in Chapter 1, feature engineering is the process of getting to the appropriate set of features from input data with the goal of producing a good machine learning model. Automated feature engineering involves four key steps, which we discuss in the subsections that follow.

Detect issues with input data and automatically flag them

Examples of this include the following:

- Detecting missing values and automatically imputing them with the most relevant technique; for example, numeric columns with mean, categorical columns with mode (most frequently occurring), and so on.

- Detecting class imbalance and automatically fixing it by applying techniques like the Synthetic Minority Oversampling Technique (SMOTE).

Drop columns that are not useful as features

Here are some examples:

No variance columns
These are columns with the same value across all rows, which are easy to detect via automation.

High cardinality columns
These are columns with different values across rows; for example, hashes, IDs, or globally unique identifiers (GUIDs). Cardinality is determined by percentage of unique values in the column.

Generate features

There are multiple techniques for generating new features from existing features. Some examples follow:

Encodings and transformations
Most machine learning algorithms require numerical input and output variables. Real-world datasets are full of text and categorical data. Data scientists convert them into numerical data by using encodings and transformations.

One-hot encoding is a popular technique to convert categorical data to integer data. You can easily automate this process. Figure 2-5 shows an example of one-hot encoding.

Original Data		One-Hot Encoding Format				
id	Color	id	White	Red	Black	Purple	Gold
1	White	1	1	0	0	0	0
2	Red	2	0	1	0	0	0
3	Black	3	0	0	1	0	0
4	Purple	4	0	0	0	1	0
5	Gold	5	0	0	0	0	1

Figure 2-5. One-hot encoding

Transformations are applied to input columns to generate interesting features. Some examples include generating "Year," "Month," "Day," "Day of week," "Day of year," "Quarter," "Week of the year," "Hour," "Minute," and "Second" for a given DateTime column. This is effective for time-series-related problems.

Other examples might generate term frequency based on unigrams, bi-grams, and tri-character-grams, and generating word embeddings for text columns.

Aggregations

Another popular technique in feature generation involves generating aggregations over multiple data records. Aggregations could be based on specific entities in the dataset (e.g., average product sales/revenue per store) or based on time (e.g., number of page views to a website in the past 7 days, 30 days, 180 days, etc.). Features generated through time-based aggregations are quite useful for time-series forecasting problems.

Select the most impactful features

Feature selection is an important step in the process because it helps to prioritize the appropriate set of input features. This becomes even more important when the number of input features is very large.

Why do we need to prioritize the proper set of input features? Why not use all the features? Here are the top benefits of feature selection:

- Faster training
- Simpler model, easier to interpret
- Reduces overfitting
- Improved model accuracy

Let's go through some different feature selection techniques. Keep in mind that you can automate all of these techniques:

Filters

According to this technique, the selection of features is independent of any machine learning algorithms. Features are selected based on their correlation with the outcome variable, as measured by statistical tests. Because the selection process is agnostic of the model, this method might not select the most useful features but is robust against overfitting. As shown in Figure 2-6, selecting the best subset of features happens before model training.

Wrappers

According to this technique, a subset of features is used to train a model. Based on the performance of the model, we decide to add or remove features from the subset and train the model again with the updated subset. This process continues until the model's performance is satisfactory. However, this technique can be computationally expensive due to multiple back-and-forth iterations. Because the selection process is tied to the model, it tends to produce more accurate results than filter methods but is more prone to overfitting. Figure 2-6 demonstrates wrapper methods.

Embedded methods

Embedded methods combine the qualities of filter and wrapper methods. Implemented by algorithms that have their own built-in feature selection methods, embedded methods are like wrappers but are less computationally expensive because there are no back-and-forth iterations. This technique is also less prone to overfitting. Figure 2-6 demonstrates embedded methods.

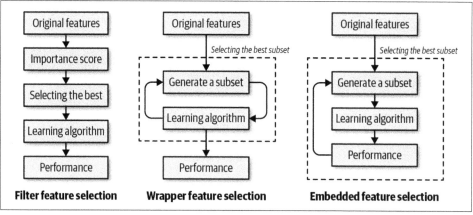

Figure 2-6. Feature selection

Selecting a Model

As discussed in the previous chapter, a machine learning model is represented by a combination of an algorithm and associated hyperparameter values. Automated Machine Learning systems follow different approaches for model selection. In this section, we discuss two categories of approaches: brute-force approaches and smarter approaches.

Brute-force approaches

This is the naïve approach of trying out all possible combinations of algorithms and hyperparameter values to find the one that produces the best model as measured by the evaluation metric. This is typically achieved by picking algorithms at random and applying *grid search* to figure out the right set of hyperparameters. One major drawback of grid search is that dimensionality suffers when the number of hyperparameters grows exponentially. With as few as four parameters, this problem can become impracticable because the number of evaluations required for this approach increases exponentially with each additional parameter, due to the curse of dimensionality.

Random search is a technique by which random combinations of the hyperparameters are used to find the best solution. In this search pattern, random combinations of parameters are considered in every iteration. Because random values are selected at each iteration, it is highly likely that the whole space has been covered due to randomness; hence the chances of finding the best model are comparatively higher than grid search. It takes a huge amount of time to cover every aspect of the combination during grid search. Random search works best if all hyperparameters are not equally important.

Figure 2-7 shows how grid search and random search work. In this example, nine sets of parameter combinations are being tried. Notice how random search manages to reach much better model performance, as shown by the dots on the "hills" at top. The topmost point on the "hill" represents the best parameter combination.

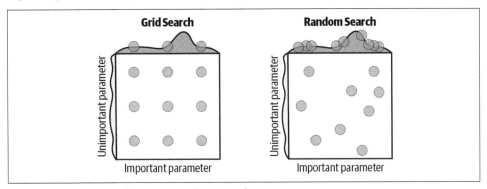

Figure 2-7. Grid search versus random search

Smarter approaches

For real-world problems, the search space is very large, and brute-force approaches will not be effective. This has led to the emergence of smarter selection and optimizations approaches, mostly powered by advanced statistics and machine learning techniques. Some of these approaches include Bayesian optimization, multiarmed bandit, and meta-learning. Here, we describe some of these at a high level (details require digging deeper and are beyond the scope of this book):

Bayesian optimization
    This method uses approximation to guess an unknown function with some prior knowledge. The goal here is to train the model based on available observations. The trained model will map to a function, which we don't know. Our task is to find the hyperparameters that maximize the learning function.

    Bayesian optimization can help you find the best model among many, speeding up the model selection process by reducing the computation task and not requiring help from a human to guess the values. This optimization technique is based on randomness and probability distributions. Figure 2-8 provides a visual description of how it works.

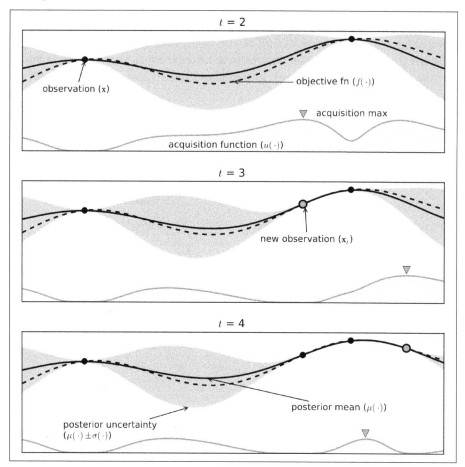

Figure 2-8. Bayesian optimization

The dotted line is our True Objective function curve. Unfortunately, we don't know this function and its equation. We are trying to approximate it by using a Gaussian process. Throughout our sample space, we draw an intuitive curve (the solid line) that fits with our observed samples (the solid dots). *t* represents different time points when we have a new observation sample. The shaded region is the Confidence region, where the point could exist. From the preceding prior knowledge, we can determine that second point as the maximum observed value. The next maximum point should be above it or equal. If we draw a horizontal line through the second point, the next maximum point should fall above this line. From the intersecting points of this line and the Confidence region, we can discard the curve samples below the line to find the maximum. In so doing, we have narrowed down our area of investigation. This same process continues with the next sampled points.

Multiarmed bandit

A multiarmed bandit is a problem in which a limited set of resources must be allocated between competing choices in a way that maximizes their expected gain when each choice's properties are only partially known at the time of allocation and might become better understood as time passes or by allocating resources to the choice.

This is a classic reinforcement learning (*https://oreil.ly/anwMJ*) problem covering the *exploration–exploitation* trade-off dilemma, modeling an agent that simultaneously attempts to acquire new knowledge (called *exploration*) and optimize its decisions based on existing knowledge (called *exploitation*). As shown in Figure 2-9, the agent attempts to balance these competing tasks to maximize its total value over the period considered.

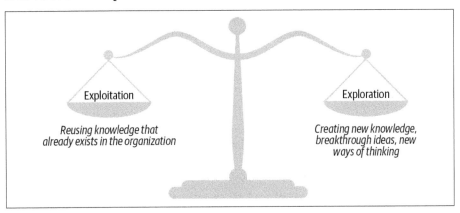

Figure 2-9. Explore versus exploit

Meta-learning

This "learning to learn." Think of this as applying machine learning to build machine learning models; hence, the term "meta" in the name. The goal of meta-learning is to train a model on a variety of learning tasks, such that it can solve new learning tasks with only a small number of training samples. Not only does this dramatically speed up and improve the design of machine learning pipelines, but also allows us to replace a fixed set of manually chosen models with novel approaches learned in a data-driven way.

With neural networks gaining popularity, meta-learning approaches have been applied to automatically design optimal neural network architectures. Known as neural architecture search (NAS), this is a popular area of research. NAS has been used to design networks that are on par with or outperform hand-designed architectures. Methods for NAS can be categorized according to the *search space*, *search strategy*, and *performance estimation strategy* used.

The search space defines the type(s) of neural networks that can be designed and optimized. The search strategy defines the approach used to explore the search space. The performance estimation strategy evaluates the performance of a possible neural network from its design (without constructing and training it).

Monitoring and Retraining

So far, we have covered the stages leading up to building a good model and how Automated Machine Learning can help with each of those stages. The last and final stage in the machine learning workflow is monitoring and retraining your model.

Model performance during training can be very different from its performance after deployment on real data. Thus, it is important to continuously measure model performance even after deployment. Poor model performance is typically caused by change in characteristics of input data over time, which is known as *data drift*. Techniques exist to automatically monitor data drift and model performance over time.

As soon as poor model performance is detected, corrective actions can be taken to minimize the damage. Corrective actions could include the following:

- Immediately take the model offline (and disable the corresponding user experience)
- Retrain the model with the latest data and deploy the retrained model

This stage is particularly critical for companies that have production dependency on machine learning models. Hence, a good Automated Machine Learning solution should have support for monitoring and training.

Bringing It All Together

Automated Machine Learning empowers users (with or without machine learning expertise) to identify an end-to-end machine learning pipeline for any problem, achieving higher accuracy while spending far less of their time. And it enables a significantly larger number of experiments to be run, resulting in faster iteration toward production-ready intelligent experiences. Given input data, it can automate the process of feature engineering, model selection, and hyperparameter tuning, as shown in Figure 2-10.

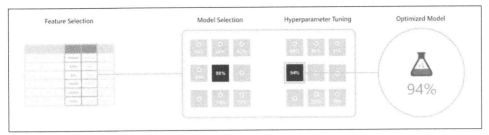

Figure 2-10. Automated Machine Learning

Automated ML

Automated ML is a capability available within the Microsoft Azure Machine Learning service. This section provides an overview of how automated ML works, whereas subsequent chapters will go into more details on how to use automated ML for your scenarios.

How Automated ML Works

Automated ML is based on a breakthrough from the Microsoft Research division (*https://arxiv.org/abs/1705.05355*). The approach combines ideas from collaborative filtering and Bayesian optimization to search an enormous space of possible machine learning pipelines intelligently and efficiently. It's essentially a recommender system for machine learning pipelines. Similar to how streaming services recommend movies for users, automated ML recommends machine learning pipelines for datasets. Figures 2-11 and 2-12 demonstrate this analogy.

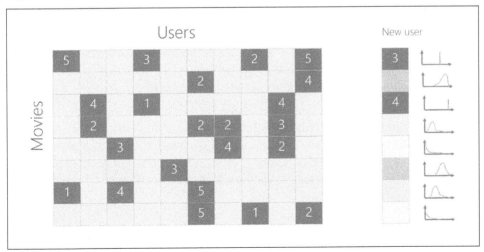

Figure 2-11. Streaming service: movie recommendation

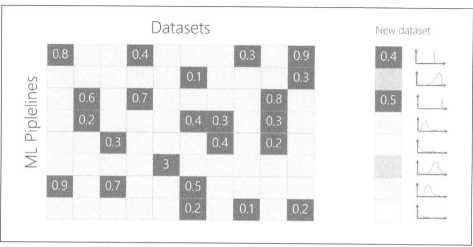

Figure 2-12. Automated ML: machine learning pipeline recommendation

As indicated by the distributions shown on the right side of Figures 2-11 and 2-12, automated ML also takes uncertainty into account, incorporating a probabilistic model to determine the best pipeline to try next. This approach allows automated ML to explore the most promising possibilities without exhaustive search, and to converge on the best pipelines for the user's data faster than competing brute-force approaches.

Preserving Privacy

Automated ML accomplishes all this without having to see the users' data, preserving privacy. As shown in Figure 2-13, users' data and execution of the machine learning pipeline both reside in the users' cloud subscription (or their local machine), for which they have complete control. Only the model performance metrics of each pipeline run are sent back to the automated ML service, which then makes an intelligent, probabilistic choice of which pipelines should be tried next.

Automated ML's probabilistic model has been trained by running hundreds of millions of experiments, each involving evaluation of a specific pipeline on a given dataset. This training now allows the automated ML service to find good solutions quickly for new problems. And the model continues to learn and improve as it runs on new machine learning tasks—even though, as just mentioned, it does not see users' data.

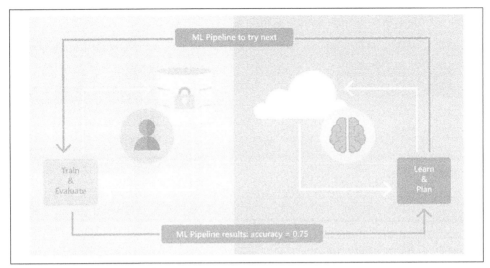

Figure 2-13. Preserving privacy

Enabling Transparency

Transparency is important for data scientists as well as other users so that they can understand what's going on, and trust the output. This is especially crucial for enterprises to use in business-critical scenarios in production.

Automated ML's heavy focus on transparency makes it easy to understand the produced machine learning pipelines, including all of the stages discussed in the previous section (e.g., data understanding, feature engineering, model selection/optimization). Users can either directly use the machine learning pipeline produced or they can customize it further.

Another aspect of transparency is to understand how the input features contribute to the outcome of the model, also known as *model explainability* or *interpretability*. Automated ML makes this easy by offering a feature importance capability. Figure 2-14 shows an example of a customer churn model for which the SupportInci dents count is the top contributing feature. This makes sense because if a customer has had a lot of support issues, the likelihood of them churning is much higher.

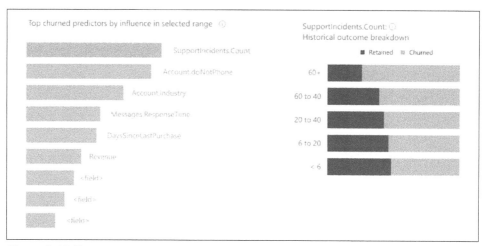

Figure 2-14. Feature importance

Guardrails

In addition to providing transparency, automated ML on Azure also offers guardrails to help users understand potential issues with their data (e.g., missing values, class imbalance) or models and help take corrective actions for improved results. We go into more detail about this in Chapter 7.

End-to-End Model Life-Cycle Management

Automated ML, being a capability of Azure Machine Learning, offers end-to-end (E2E) model life-cycle management, including easy deployment, monitoring, drift analysis, and retraining through integration with ML operationalization (MLOps) capability of Azure Machine Learning. Figure 2-15 shows this E2E flow.

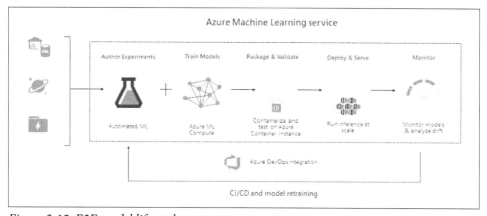

Figure 2-15. E2E model life-cycle management

Conclusion

In this chapter, you learned what Automated Machine Learning is, generally speaking, and how it can help with every stage of building a good machine learning model to solve real-world problems. We also provided a brief overview of how the Azure Machine Learning capability, automated ML, works behind the scenes to build good machine learning models and enable trust by allowing transparency and preserving data privacy.

In subsequent chapters, we'll cover different aspects of what we touched upon here, and provide hands-on practice and sample scenarios to help you use automated ML in your work.

## PART II

Automated ML on Azure

In this part, you will begin using automated ML on Azure. You'll also learn how some machine learning techniques can be used with automated ML.

## CHAPTER 3

Getting Started with Microsoft Azure Machine Learning and Automated ML

In Chapter 2, we explained the concept of Automated Machine Learning and provided a brief overview of the automated ML tool on Microsoft Azure Machine Learning. In this chapter, we look at how to get started with Azure Machine Learning and, subsequently, automated ML. Before going into details of automated ML, we'll first discuss some of the common challenges that enterprises face in their machine learning projects, to better understand these issues.

The Machine Learning Process

When solving problems with machine learning, we begin with a problem statement in terms of what we are trying to optimize. Next, we look for a dataset that will help us solve the problem. We begin looking at the data and use a data manipulation library like Pandas. We look at missing values, distribution of data, and errors in the data. We try to join multiple datasets. When we think we have a good enough dataset to get underway, we split it into train, test, and validation datasets, typically in a ratio of 70:20:10. This helps avoid overfitting, which basically means we're not using the same dataset for training and testing. We use the train dataset to train the machine learning algorithm. The test dataset is used for testing the machine learning model after training is complete, to ascertain how well the algorithm performed.

We establish a metric to determine algorithm performance and keep iterating until we get a good algorithm. Then we use the validation dataset to check the algorithm's performance. Sometimes, the validation dataset might not be in the main dataset, in which case we can split the original dataset for training and testing in an 80:20 ratio. All of these datasets should be representative samples of the main dataset to avoid *skewed data* (also known as *bias*). As you can see, this process is iterative and can be time-consuming. Figure 3-1 shows a summary of the manual process.

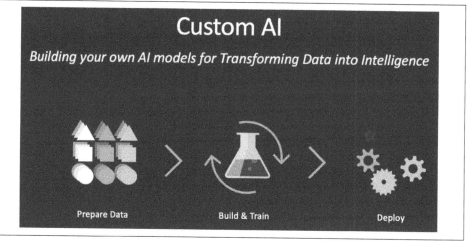

Figure 3-1. Manual process for custom artificial intelligence

Let's look at some of the other challenges a data scientist can face when embarking on a machine learning project.

Collaboration and Monitoring

Data scientists in the enterprise can work solo or in teams. Nowadays, machine learning projects are more complicated, and data scientists often collaborate. However, it might not be easy for data scientists to share results and review code.

Other challenges that data scientists face when working together are how to track the machine learning experiments and then track the history of multiple iterations (runs) within each experiment. There are additional challenges to having a training environment that can scale horizontally and vertically. When we need more nodes in a cluster, we want to scale it horizontally, and when we need more CPU or memory, we scale each node vertically.

Deployment

After the trained model satisfies the business criteria, the next step is to operationalize it so that we can use it for predictions. This is also known as *deployment of the model*. A model can be deployed as a web service for real-time scoring or as a batch-scoring model for scoring in bulk. Figure 3-2 shows a summary of the steps a data scientist might perform, from training to deployment. Now, let's understand how Azure Machine Learning and automated ML help address some of these challenges.

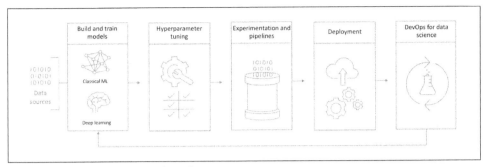

Figure 3-2. The steps for machine learning

Setting Up an Azure Machine Learning Workspace for Automated ML

The Azure Machine Learning service helps data scientists track experiments and iterations (runs) in a cloud-based workspace. It is a machine learning platform designed to help with end-to-end (E2E) machine learning.

To use the Azure Machine Learning service (including the Azure Machine Learning SDK, and automated ML), you must have an Azure Machine Learning workspace. This workspace resides in your Azure subscription and you can use it as a single collaborative place to track experiments and do more things. Anyone with owner or contributor access to the resource group can create the workspace in an Azure resource group. You can create it using Microsoft Azure portal or using the Python SDK. Later in this chapter, we review in detail the steps of installing the SDK.

When creating the workspace for the first time, you need to register a few resource providers (RP) in the Azure subscription. Let's register the RPs needed to use the Azure Machine Learning workspace. You can search for this RPs in the Azure portal under your subscription. Here are the steps to do this:

1. Open the Azure portal, and then go to your subscription, as shown in Figure 3-3.

Figure 3-3. Subscription overview

2. On the left side of the pane, browse to "Resource providers," as shown in Figure 3-4.

Figure 3-4. Resource providers list

3. In the filter, in the Search box, type "machinelearning," and then register the Machine Learning RPs, as shown in Figure 3-5.

Figure 3-5. Machine learning–related resource providers

4. Register the KeyVault, ContainerRegistry, and ContainerInstance RPs, as shown in Figures 3-6 and 3-7.

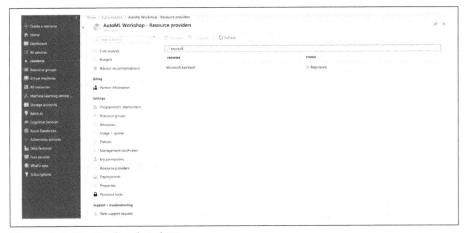

Figure 3-6. KeyVault-related RPs

Figure 3-7. Containers-related RPs

Now we're ready to create an Azure ML workspace. To do this, we need Contributor or Owner access to the Azure resource group. After we have confirmed the appropriate access, let's create the Azure Machine Learning workspace:

1. Go to the Azure portal and search for "machine learning service workspaces," as shown in Figure 3-8.

Figure 3-8. Going to the machine learning workspace on Azure portal

2. Fill in the required details in the pane, as shown in Figures 3-9 through 3-11.

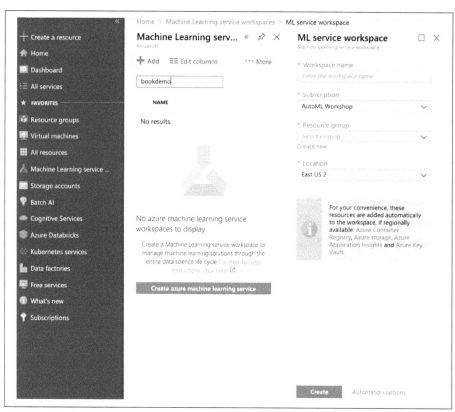

Figure 3-9. The Azure Machine Learning service creation pane

You can choose an existing resource group or create a new one.

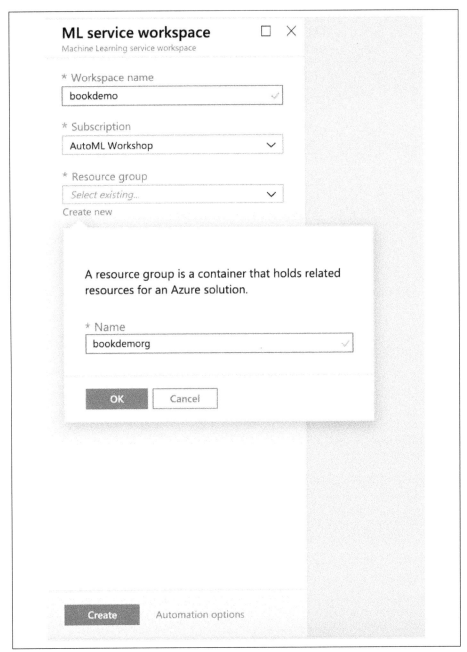

Figure 3-10. The Azure resource group creation pane

Click Create when you have made all your selections.

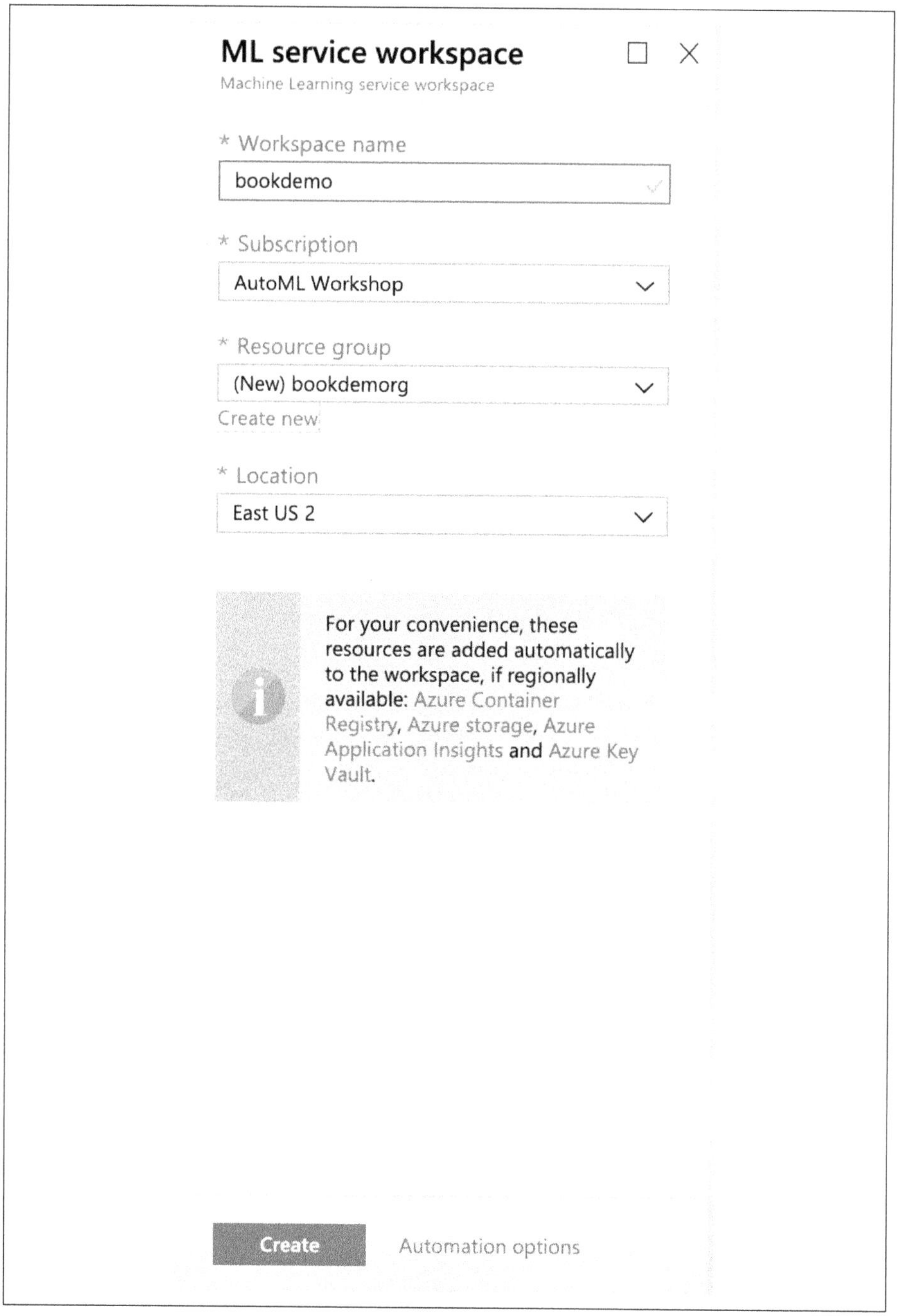

ML service workspace
Machine Learning service workspace

□ ✕

* Workspace name

bookdemo

* Subscription

AutoML Workshop ∨

* Resource group

(New) bookdemorg ∨

Create new

* Location

East US 2 ∨

ⓘ For your convenience, these resources are added automatically to the workspace, if regionally available: Azure Container Registry, Azure storage, Azure Application Insights and Azure Key Vault.

Create   Automation options

Figure 3-11. The Azure Machine Learning workspace creation pane

3. In the upper part of the notification pane that then opens, click the bell icon (Figure 3-12) to go to the newly created Azure Machine Learning workspace.

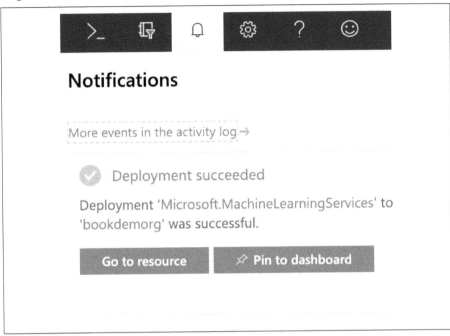

Figure 3-12. Azure Machine Learning workspace notification pane

4. As shown in Figure 3-13, the main page of the Azure Machine Learning workspace shows you how to get started and all of the assets that are a part of the workspace. When we run our automated ML experiment, the details will show up in the Experiments section.

After you create this workspace, you can use it for training, deployment, and more machine learning–related activities. For the remainder of this chapter, we focus on using automated ML.

Figure 3-13. Azure Machine Learning workspace overview page

Azure Notebooks

There are multiple ways a data scientist or artificial intelligence (AI) developer can use automated ML. It comes packaged as part of the Azure Machine Learning SDK. It can be installed in any Python environment as a PyPi package.

Here we use Azure Notebooks (a Jupyter environment in the cloud) to run an E2E experiment with automated ML. When used with Azure Notebooks, the SDK is pre-installed in the environment. Let's create a project:

1. Start Azure Notebooks by going to *https://notebooks.azure.com*, as shown in Figure 3-14. Click the Try It Now button and sign in.

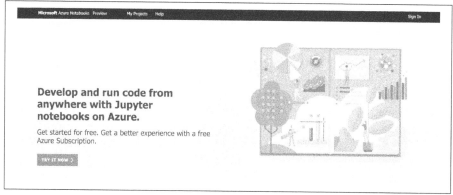

Figure 3-14. Azure Notebooks home screen

2. From your profile page, you can view the Azure Notebooks projects (Figure 3-15).

Figure 3-15. An example Azure Notebooks profile page

3. Run the compute as your notebook server, as depicted in Figure 3-16.

Figure 3-16. Associating a Jupyter server for the compute type

4. Once you open the notebook (see Figure 3-17), it spins up the Jupyter kernel. You can execute the code in the cell by pressing Shift + Enter.

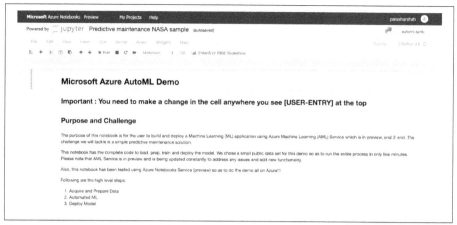

Figure 3-17. A Jupyter notebook

5. As shown in Figures 3-18 and 3-19, you begin by authorizing the environment to access the Azure subscription and thus the Azure Machine Learning workspace that you created earlier.

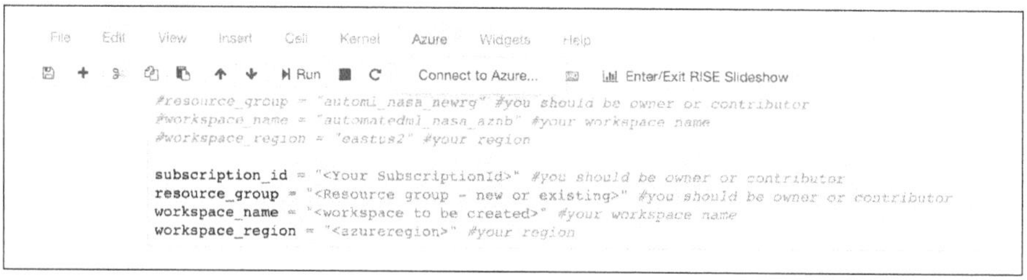

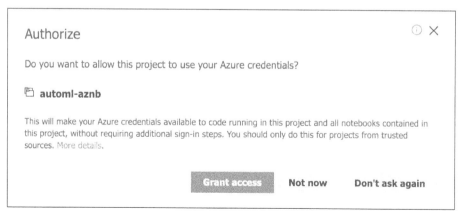

Figure 3-18. Connecting to Azure

Authorize

Do you want to allow this project to use your Azure credentials?

automl-aznb

This will make your Azure credentials available to code running in this project and all notebooks contained in this project, without requiring additional sign-in steps. You should only do this for projects from trusted sources. More details.

Grant access   **Not now**   **Don't ask again**

Figure 3-19. Authorizing the Azure Machine Learning workspace

6. Now, instantiate the Azure Machine Learning workspace by providing the subscription, resource group, and workspace name as shown in Figures 3-20 and 3-21. Begin by importing the libraries and then use the `get` method to instantiate the workspace object, which can then be used by automated ML and other related activities.

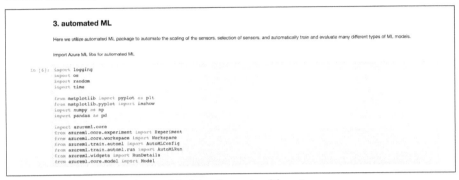

Figure 3-20. Importing Azure Machine Learning libraries

```
# Import the Workspace class and check the Azure ML SDK version.
from azureml.core import Workspace

ws = Workspace.get(name = workspace_name,
                   subscription_id = subscription_id,
                   resource_group = resource_group)
```

Figure 3-21. Instantiating the Azure Machine Learning workspace

7. Define an experiment within the Azure Machine Learning workspace to get started with automated ML, as shown in Figure 3-22.

Define the experiment name

```
In [9]:  # Choose a name for the experiment and specify the project folder.
         experiment_name = 'automl-predictive-rul'
         project_folder = './sample_projects/automl-demo-predmain'

         experiment = Experiment(ws, experiment_name)

         output = {}
         output['SDK version'] = azureml.core.VERSION
         output['Subscription ID'] = ws.subscription_id
         output['Workspace Name'] = ws.name
         output['Resource Group'] = ws.resource_group
         output['Location'] = ws.location
         output['Project Directory'] = project_folder
         output['Experiment Name'] = experiment.name
         pd.set_option('display.max_colwidth', -1)
         pd.DataFrame(data = output, index = [''] ).T
```

Out[9]:

Experiment Name	automl-predictive-rul
Location	eastus2
Project Directory	./sample_projects/automl-demo-predmain
Resource Group	automl_aznb_ps
SDK version	1.0.17
Subscription ID	ba7979f7-d040-49c9-af1a-7414402bf622
Workspace Name	aml_aznb_demo

Figure 3-22. Defining an experiment in the Azure Machine Learning workspace

8. From the dataset that will be used for automated ML training, we create the DataFrames for the feature columns and prediction label. These DataFrames are represented as X and y in the automated ML configuration. The configuration takes various other parameters, as shown in Figures 3-23 and 3-24.

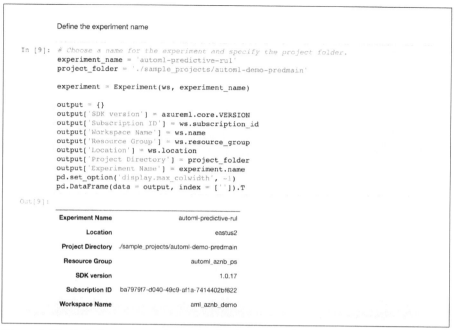

Figure 3-23. Configuration parameters for an automated ML experiment in the Azure Machine Learning workspace

In addition to the experiment type, these parameters define the constraints that help control the time it takes and the money we spend on training. Details of these parameters are available in the official Azure documentation (*http://bit.ly/2lCRoUy*).

```
In [18]: ##Notebook compute
         Automl_config = AutoMLConfig(task = 'regression',
                                      primary_metric = 'r2_score',
                                      iteration_timeout_minutes = 15,
                                      iterations = 10,
                                      max_cores_per_iteration = 1,
                                      preprocess = False,
                                      experiment_exit_score = 0.985,
                                      X = X_train,
                                      y = y_train,
                                      X_valid = X_valid,
                                      y_valid = y_valid,
                                      #n_cross_validations = 3, # uncomment this if not specifying valid dataframe
                                      debug_log = 'automl_errors.log',
                                      verbosity=logging.ERROR,
                                      path=project_folder)
```

Figure 3-24. Configuring an automated ML experiment

Submit this training and monitor the progress of the experiment in the notebook by using a widget, or through the Azure portal in your Azure Machine Learning workspace, as shown in Figures 3-25 through 3-27. This shows the metric score, status, and duration of the experiment run. These metrics can be useful to find what automated ML tried and the result of each iteration.

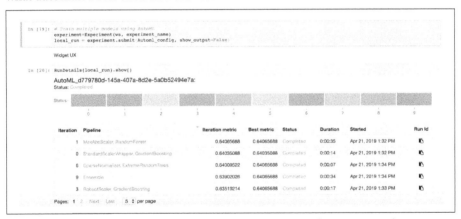

Figure 3-25. Monitoring the progress of an experiment in the Azure Machine Learning workspace

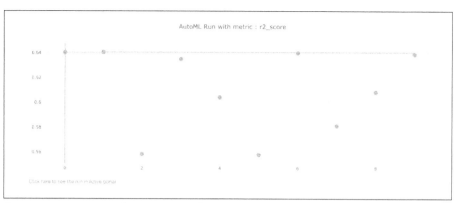

Figure 3-26. Metrics of an automated ML run in the Azure Machine Learning workspace

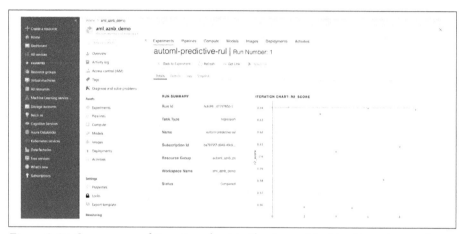

Figure 3-27. Summary and iteration chart in the Azure Machine Learning workspace

9. We can explore details in the child runs (iteration) by checking graphs of the true value and predicted value, as shown in Figures 3-28 and 3-29.

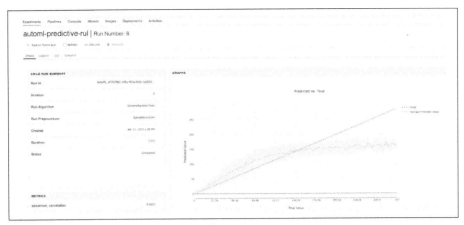

Figure 3-28. Prediction versus true value

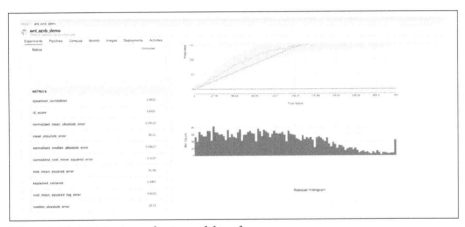

Figure 3-29. Metrics to evaluate model performance

10. You can export the trained model from any of the child runs, as shown in Figure 3-30. Using Azure Machine Learning, you can deploy this model to the cloud or edge for making predictions. You also can deploy it to another environment of your choice. You can take advantage of the benefits of containerizing the model and then deploying it as a real-time web service or as a batch service using Azure Machine Learning. (We examine deployment in Chapter 5.)

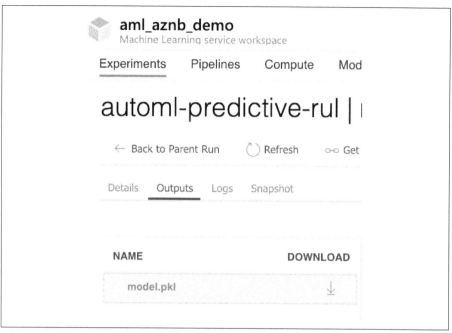

Figure 3-30. Downloading and deploying a model file

11. Alternatively, after the training is complete, you can select the best model writing Python code as shown in Figure 3-31.

```
We now get the best model

In [21]:  # find the run with the highest accuracy value.
          best_run, fitted_model = local_run.get_output()
          print(best_run)

          Run(Experiment: automl-predictive-rul,
          Id: AutoML_d779780d-145a-407a-8d2e-5a0b52494e7a_1,
          Type: None,
          Status: Completed)
```

Figure 3-31. Selecting the model from the best run

12. When you go to the main experiments page in your Azure Machine Learning workspace, you can look at all the experiments that you have run as well as their child runs. The portal automatically sorts the child runs based on the metric you are optimizing. In Figure 3-32, you can see a summary of the experiment run. It has various panes to show the run config and the run results. The best pipeline is shown at the top in Figure 3-33.

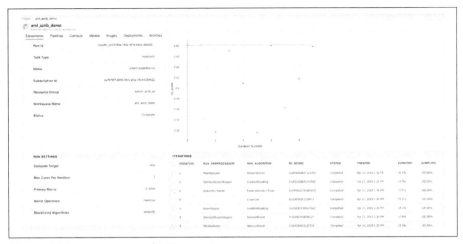

Figure 3-32. An automated ML experiment run summary

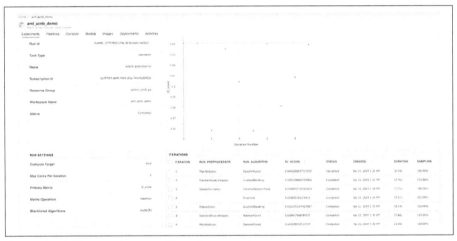

Figure 3-33. Run results sorted based on metric

Notebook VM

As of this writing, a new cloud-based notebook server is available in preview. This secure, cloud-based Azure workstation provides a Jupyter notebook server, Jupyter-Lab, and a fully prepared machine learning environment. You can learn more about it in the Azure Machine Learning Notebooks documentation (*https://oreil.ly/e-56d*).

Conclusion

In this chapter, you learned about the Azure Machine Learning workspace and how to get started with automated ML by using Azure Notebooks. In Chapter 8, you'll use more coding environments to run automated ML experiments.

## CHAPTER 4

Feature Engineering and Automated Machine Learning

Feature engineering is one of the most important parts of the data science process. If you ask data scientists to break down the time spent in each stage of the data science process, you'll often hear that they spend a significant amount of time understanding and exploring the data, and doing *feature engineering*. Most experienced data scientists do not jump into model building. Rather, they first spend time doing feature engineering.

But what is feature engineering? With feature engineering, you can transform your original data into a form that is more easily understood by the machine learning algorithms. For example, you might perform data processing, add new features (e.g., additional data columns that combine values from existing columns), or you might transform the features from their original domain to a different domain. You might also remove features that are not useful or relevant to the model. When doing feature engineering, you will generate new features, transform existing features, or select a subset of features.

To illustrate how you can transform features, let's consider a simple example of working with *categorical features* (otherwise known as *categorical variables*). Suppose that you have a dataset for an airline customer program with a feature called Status, which determines the status of the customers (e.g., based on how often the customer flies, total miles traveled, and others). Status contains the following five unique values: New, Silver, Gold, Platinum, and Diamond. Because some of the machine learning algorithms can work only with numerical variables, you will need to transform the feature. A common approach is to use *one-hot encoding*, as shown in Table 4-1.

Table 4-1. One-hot encoding

Status		New	Silver	Gold	Platinum	Diamond
Gold		0	0	1	0	0
Silver		0	1	0	0	0
New	⇨	1	0	0	0	0
Platinum		0	0	0	1	0
Silver		0	1	0	0	0
Gold		0	0	1	0	0

Another important aspect of feature engineering is taking advantage of domain expertise. You might consider working with a person who has relevant domain expertise when doing feature engineering—the inputs from the domain expert will be invaluable when working toward the goal of delivering a high-quality model.

Transparency and *explainability* are important considerations when training machine learning models. Hence, doing feature engineering properly will contribute toward having high-performing models that can be explained.

Chapter 7 provides a detailed discussion on how Azure Machine Learning gives you the tools to understand the models generated, the relative importance of features, and more.

When performing feature engineering, data scientists often ask themselves the following questions:

- Which features in the dataset are irrelevant to the model? For example, your data might contain an Identifier (ID) column. Though this column is useful when combining data from several datasets (e.g., joining two datasets based on an employee_id), the ID column is not used in any way when training the model.

- Can we combine one or more features to create new features that will be even more useful?

- For some of the classes that are sparse (i.e., those that contain significantly fewer observations), can we group them to create more meaningful classes?

In this chapter, we focus on how to use the auto-featurization capabilities provided in the automated ML tool that is a part of Microsoft Azure Machine Learning. You will learn how auto-featurization works for classification, regression, and forecasting tasks. In addition, we share pointers and resources that enable you to go more in-depth with feature engineering. Before we dive into the auto-featurization performed by automated ML, let's look at the data preprocessing methods that are available.

Data Preprocessing Methods Available in Automated ML

Depending on the type of machine learning task (e.g., classification, regression, forecasting), different types of data preprocessing are performed. When you use automated ML and submit an experiment, you will notice that each iteration performs a different type of data preprocessing.

For example, you will notice that your data is scaled, or normalized, when it is relevant. When features have different ranges, scaling and normalization helps. Table 4-2 shows the scaling and normalization steps performed by automated ML.

Table 4-2. Data preprocessing performed by automated ML

Scaling and normalization	Description
MinMaxScalar (*https://oreil.ly/FBzE4*)	Each feature is transformed by scaling to the minimum and maximum for that column.
MaxAbsScaler (*https://oreil.ly/pGvd2*)	Each feature is scaled by using the maximum absolute value.
RobustScalar (*https://oreil.ly/AUlqU*)	Each feature is scaled by using the values from quantile range.
PCA (*https://oreil.ly/6wb1B*)	Linear dimensionality reduction using singular value decomposition (SVD) of the data to project it to a lower dimensional space.
TruncatedSVDWrapper (*https://oreil.ly/mNQ86*)	Uses truncated SVD to do linear dimensionality reduction. Unlike principal component analysis (PCA), the data is not centered before SVD is computed. Note: This enables it to work efficiently with `scipy.sparse` matrices.
SparseNormalizer (*https://oreil.ly/qmKyn*)	Each sample that contains one or more nonzero components is independently rescaled, enabling the norm (L1 or L2) to equal one.

> For more details on how data is preprocessed in Azure Machine Learning, see this section (*https://oreil.ly/vEGJu*) of the Microsoft Azure documentation.

Auto-Featurization for Automated ML

Let's get started with using auto-featurization. By now, you should be familiar with how to set up the automated ML configuration object. Let's recap how you set up the automated ML experiment. In the code example that follows, you first define the `AutoMLConfig` object. Next, specify the name of the experiment, number of iterations to run, the logging granularity, and more. After you have defined the `AutoMLConfig` object, submit the experiment by using `experiment.submit(...)`:

```
import time

automl_settings = {
    "name": "AutoML_Book_CH07_FeatureEngineering_{0}".format(time.time()),
    "task": "regression",
    "iteration_timeout_minutes": 10,
    "iterations": 10,
    "max_cores_per_iteration": 1,
    "primary_metric": 'r2_score',
    "max_concurrent_iterations": 10,
    "experiment_exit_score": 0.985,
    "debug_log": "automl_ch07_errors{0}.log".format(time.time()),
    "verbosity": logging.ERROR
}
# Local compute
Automl_config = AutoMLConfig(
                preprocess = False,
                X = X_train,
                y = y_train,
                X_valid = X_valid,
                y_valid = y_valid,
                path=project_folder,
                **automl_settings)

# Training the model
experiment=Experiment(ws, experiment_name)
local_run = experiment.submit(Automl_config, show_output=True)
```

After you submit the experiment, notice the data processing that has been performed in each iteration (see the output in Figure 4-1). From iteration 0 to 7, you can see that each iteration shows what type of data preprocessing has been performed. For example, in iteration 0, we can see that the StandardScalerWrapper is used. In iteration 3, the RobustScaler is used.

In the code shown earlier, in which you defined the AutoMLConfig object, notice that one of the properties, preprocess, is set to False. You can also set preprocess = True to turn on advanced data preprocessing. This makes it possible for you to use both data preprocessing and auto-featurization.

The type of auto-featurization performed depends on the machine learning task you're planning. For example, if you use automated ML for classification and regression, auto-featurization might include dropping features with a high cardinality, or low variance. If you use automated ML for forecasting, additional features might be generated for DateTime, or relation of the DateTime to holidays in various countries.

```
# Training the predictive maintenance model
experiment=Experiment(ws, experiment_name)
local_run = experiment.submit(Automl_config, show_output=True)

Running on local machine
Parent Run ID: AutoML_0dc694bd-da06-47aa-b4f4-077d1696d553
Current status: ModelSelection. Beginning model selection.

************************************************************************************
ITERATION: The iteration being evaluated.
PIPELINE: A summary description of the pipeline being evaluated.
DURATION: Time taken for the current iteration.
METRIC: The result of computing score on the fitted pipeline.
BEST: The best observed score thus far.
************************************************************************************

 ITERATION   PIPELINE                                            DURATION    METRIC    BEST
         0   StandardScalerWrapper LightGBM                      0:00:37     0.6161    0.6161
         1   MaxAbsScaler LightGBM                               0:00:19     0.6186    0.6186
         2   StandardScalerWrapper ExtremeRandomTrees            0:00:11     0.4183    0.6186
         3   RobustScaler LightGBM                               0:00:18     0.6165    0.6186
         4   StandardScalerWrapper LightGBM                      0:00:14     0.4834    0.6186
         5   StandardScalerWrapper LightGBM                      0:00:11     0.6220    0.6220
         6   StandardScalerWrapper ElasticNet                    0:00:11     0.4773    0.6220
         7   StandardScalerWrapper ExtremeRandomTrees            0:00:11     0.5301    0.6220
         8   VotingEnsemble                                      0:00:37     0.6255    0.6255
         9   StackEnsemble                                       0:00:43     0.6254    0.6255
```

Figure 4-1. Data preprocessing using automated ML

Table 4-3 presents the auto-featurization features used by automated ML.

Table 4-3. Auto-featurization performed by automated ML

Preprocessing and auto-featurization	Description
Drop high-cardinality or no variance features	Drop these from training and validation sets, including features with all values missing, same value across all rows, or with extremely high-cardinality (e.g., hashes, IDs, or GUIDs).
Impute missing values	For numerical features, impute with average of values in the column. For categorical features, impute with most frequent value.
Generate additional features	For DateTime features: Year, Month, Day, Day of week, Day of year, Quarter, Week of the year, Hour, Minute, Second. For Text features: Term frequency based on unigrams, bi-grams, and tri-character-grams.
Transform and encode	Numeric features with few unique values are transformed into categorical features. One-hot encoding is performed for low cardinality categorical; for high cardinality, one-hot-hash encoding.
Word embeddings	Text featurizer that converts vectors of text tokens into sentence vectors using a pretrained model. In a given document, each word's embedding vector is aggregated to produce a document feature vector.
Target encodings	For categorical features, maps each category to averaged target value for regression problems. For classification problems, maps each category to the class probability for each class. Frequency-based weighting and k-fold cross-validation is applied to reduce overfitting of the mapping and noise caused by sparse data categories.

Preprocessing and auto-featurization	Description
Text target encoding	For text input, a stacked linear model with bag-of-words is used to generate the probability of each class.
Weight of Evidence (WoE)	Calculates WoE as a measure of correlation of categorical columns to the target column. It is calculated as the log of the ratio of in-class versus out-of-class probabilities. This step outputs one numerical feature column per class and removes the need to explicitly impute missing values and outlier treatment.
Cluster distance	Trains a k-means clustering model on all numerical columns. Outputs k new features, one new numerical feature per cluster, containing the distance of each sample to the centroid of each cluster.

Auto-Featurization for Classification and Regression

To show auto-featurization in action, let's work through a predictive maintenance model using the NASA Turbofan Engine Degradation Simulation dataset. In this example, even though we show how regression is used to predict the remaining useful lifetime (RUL) value for the turbofan engine, we can apply the same approach to classification problems as well.

To do this, let's first download the dataset using the code block that follows. After you download the dataset, you extract the file into the data folder, and read the training data file, *data/train_FD004.txt*. Then, you add the column names for the 26 features. Use the following code to do this:

```
# Download the NASA Turbofan Engine Degradation Simulation Dataset
import requests, zipfile, io
import pandas as pd
nasa_dataset_url = https://ti.arc.nasa.gov/c/6/
r = requests.get(nasa_dataset_url)

z = zipfile.ZipFile(io.BytesIO(r.content))
z.extractall("data/")
train = pd.read_csv("data/train_FD004.txt", delimiter="\s|\s\s",
          index_col=False, engine='python',
          names=['unit','cycle','os1','os2','os3',
               'sm1','sm2','sm3','sm4','sm5','sm6','sm7','sm8',
               'sm9','sm10', 'sm11','sm12','sm13','sm14','sm15','sm16',
               'sm17','sm18','sm19','sm20','sm21'])
```

An important part of the data science process is to explore the dataset. Since we use this dataset in other chapters, we won't explore it here. In addition, we'll omit the steps needed to create the Azure Machine Learning experiment and set up the AutoML Config object (shown earlier) and proceed directly to exploring the differences and quality of results when preprocess is set to different values (i.e., True or False).

Before we do that, let's define the utility functions that will be useful in the exploration. We will create two utility functions: print_model() (Example 4-1), and print_engineered_features() (Example 4-2). These two utility functions are used to print the pipelines for a model, and the features that are generated during auto-featurization, respectively, as shown in the following examples.

Example 4-1. print_model

```
from pprint import pprint

def print_model(run, model, prefix=""):
    print(run)
    print("---------")

for step in model.steps:
    print(prefix + step[0])
    if hasattr(step[1], 'estimators') and hasattr(step[1], 'weights'):
        pprint({'estimators': list(e[0] for e in step[1].estimators),
            'weights': step[1].weights})

        print()
        for estimator in step[1].estimators:
            print_model(estimator[1], estimator[0]+ ' - ')
    elif hasattr(step[1], '_base_learners') and
        hasattr(step[1], '_meta_learner'):

        print("\nMeta Learner")
        pprint(step[1]._meta_learner)
        print()

        for estimator in step[1]._base_learners:
            print_model(estimator[1], estimator[0]+ ' - ')
    else:
        pprint(step[1].get_params())
        print()
```

Example 4-2. print_engineered_features

```
from pprint import pprint
import pandas as pd
# Function to pretty print the engineered features
def print_engineered_features(features_summary):
    print(pd.DataFrame(features_summary,
        columns=["RawFeatureName",
            "TypeDetected",
            "Dropped",
            "EngineeredFeatureCount",
            "Tranformations"]))
```

Now that we have defined the two utility functions, let's explore two iterations for an experiment in which preprocess is set to False, and the data preprocessing shown in the outputs are similar. (Figure 4-1 shows the output after the experiment is submitted.) Iterations 4 and 5 of the experiment use the same data processing technique

(StandardScalerWrapper) and the same machine learning algorithm (LightGBM). What's the difference between the two iterations, and why do they show two different R2 score values? Iteration 5 (R2 score of 0.6220) seems to have performed better than iteration 4 (R2 score of 0.4834).

Using local_run.get_output(), we extracted the run and models that have been trained for iterations 4 and 5. The run information is stored in *explore_run1* and *explore_run2*, and the model details are stored in *explore_model1* and *explore_model2*:

```
explore_run1, explore_model1 = local_run.get_output(iteration = 4)
explore_run2, explore_model2 = local_run.get_output(iteration = 5)
```

After you have extracted the run information and model details, let's look at them closely. From the output for iterations 4 and 5 shown, you will notice the hyperparameter values are different (e.g., max_bin, max_depth, learning_rate, reg_alpha, reg_lambda, and others). These hyperparameter values are determined by the automated ML meta-model that has been trained to decide which machine learning pipeline will be most relevant to the dataset (see Examples 4-3 and 4-4).

 See Chapter 2 for more on how Automated Machine Learning works.

Example 4-3. Iteration 4 run and model information

```
Run(Experiment: automl-predictive-rul-ch07,
Id: AutoML_0dc694bd-da06-47aa-b4f4-077d1696d553_4,
Type: None,
Status: Completed)
---
StandardScalerWrapper
{'class_name': 'StandardScaler',
 'copy': True,
 'module_name': 'sklearn.preprocessing.data',
 'with_mean': False,
 'with_std': True}

LightGBMRegressor
{'boosting_type': 'gbdt',
 'class_weight': None,
 'colsample_bytree': 0.7000000000000001,
 'importance_type': 'split',
 'learning_rate': 0.1894742105263158,
 'max_bin': 7,
 'max_depth': 3,
 'min_child_samples': 139,
 'min_child_weight': 0.001,
```

```
 'min_split_gain': 0.9473684210526315,
 'n_estimators': 800,
 'n_jobs': 1,
 'num_leaves': 7,
 'objective': None,
 'random_state': None,
 'reg_alpha': 0.075,
 'reg_lambda': 0.6,
 'silent': True,
 'subsample': 0.7999999999999999,
 'subsample_for_bin': 200000,
 'subsample_freq': 0,
 'verbose': -1}
```

Example 4-4. Iteration 5 run and model information

```
Run(Experiment: automl-predictive-rul-ch07,
Id: AutoML_0dc694bd-da06-47aa-b4f4-077d1696d553_5,
Type: None,
Status: Completed)
---
StandardScalerWrapper
{'class_name': 'StandardScaler',
 'copy': True,
 'module_name': 'sklearn.preprocessing.data',
 'with_mean': True,
 'with_std': True}

LightGBMRegressor
{'boosting_type': 'gbdt',
 'class_weight': None,
 'colsample_bytree': 0.5,
 'importance_type': 'split',
 'learning_rate': 0.1789484210526316,
 'max_bin': 255,
 'max_depth': 9,
 'min_child_samples': 194,
 'min_child_weight': 0.001,
 'min_split_gain': 0.9473684210526315,
 'n_estimators': 100,
 'n_jobs': 1,
 'num_leaves': 127,
 'objective': None,
 'random_state': None,
 'reg_alpha': 1.125,
 'reg_lambda': 0.75,
 'silent': True,
 'subsample': 0.7,
 'subsample_for_bin': 200000,
 'subsample_freq': 0,
 'verbose': -1}
```

Next, let's look at the names of the engineered features. To do this, you can use the function `get_engineered_feature_names ()`. The code shows how you retrieve the best run and model by using `local_run.get_output()` and then extract the names of the engineered features:

```
best_run, fitted_model = local_run.get_output()
fitted_model.named_steps['datatransformer']. get_engineered_feature_names ()
```

Figure 4-2 shows the output. In this example, you will see that the engineered features are derived from using the `MeanImputer` transform on the existing features. No additional features have been added.

```
Out[52]:  ['C1_MeanImputer',
           'C2_MeanImputer',
           'C3_MeanImputer',
           'C4_MeanImputer',
           'C5_MeanImputer',
           'C6_MeanImputer',
           'C7_MeanImputer',
           'C8_MeanImputer',
           'C9_MeanImputer',
           'C10_MeanImputer',
           'C11_MeanImputer',
           'C12_MeanImputer',
           'C13_MeanImputer',
           'C14_MeanImputer',
           'C15_MeanImputer',
           'C16_MeanImputer',
           'C17_MeanImputer',
           'C18_MeanImputer',
           'C19_MeanImputer',
           'C20_MeanImputer',
           'C21_MeanImputer',
           'C22_MeanImputer',
           'C23_MeanImputer',
           'C24_MeanImputer']
```

Figure 4-2. Names of engineered features

Let's dive deeper and look at more details about the engineered features. To do this, use the `get_featurization_summary()` function. The utility function `print_engineered_features()` that we defined earlier will enable us to pretty-print the output and make it easier to read.

Figure 4-3 shows the summary of the engineered features. For each original feature, you will see that the `MeanImputer` transform is applied to it and that the count for new engineered features is 1. You will also observe that no features were dropped when data preprocessing and auto-featurization are performed:

```
# Get the summary of the engineered features
features_summary =
    fitted_model.named_steps['datatransformer'].get_featurization_summary()
print_engineered_features(features_summary)
```

	RawFeatureName	TypeDetected	Dropped	EngineeredFeatureCount	Tranformations
0	C1	Numeric	No	1	[MeanImputer]
1	C2	Numeric	No	1	[MeanImputer]
2	C3	Numeric	No	1	[MeanImputer]
3	C4	Numeric	No	1	[MeanImputer]
4	C5	Numeric	No	1	[MeanImputer]
5	C6	Numeric	No	1	[MeanImputer]
6	C7	Numeric	No	1	[MeanImputer]
7	C8	Numeric	No	1	[MeanImputer]
8	C9	Numeric	No	1	[MeanImputer]
9	C10	Numeric	No	1	[MeanImputer]
10	C11	Numeric	No	1	[MeanImputer]
11	C12	Numeric	No	1	[MeanImputer]
12	C13	Numeric	No	1	[MeanImputer]
13	C14	Numeric	No	1	[MeanImputer]
14	C15	Numeric	No	1	[MeanImputer]
15	C16	Numeric	No	1	[MeanImputer]
16	C17	Numeric	No	1	[MeanImputer]
17	C18	Numeric	No	1	[MeanImputer]
18	C19	Numeric	No	1	[MeanImputer]
19	C20	Numeric	No	1	[MeanImputer]
20	C21	Numeric	No	1	[MeanImputer]
21	C22	Numeric	No	1	[MeanImputer]
22	C23	Numeric	No	1	[MeanImputer]
23	C24	Numeric	No	1	[MeanImputer]

Figure 4-3. Summary of engineered features

Auto-Featurization for Time-Series Forecasting

In this next example, we show how data preprocessing and auto-featurization is performed for a time-series dataset, in which the data type for some of the features is DateTime.

Let's begin by downloading the sample Energy Demand dataset (Figure 4-4 shows the output from running the code):

```
import requests, zipfile, io

# Download the data for energy demand forecasting

nyc_energy_data_url =
"https://raw.githubusercontent.com/Azure/MachineLearningNotebooks/master/
    how-to-use-azureml/automated-machine-learning/
```

```
           forecasting-energy-demand/nyc_energy.csv"

r = requests.get(nyc_energy_data_url)
open('data/nyc_energy.csv', 'wb').write(r.content)

data = pd.read_csv('data/nyc_energy.csv', parse_dates=['timeStamp'])
data.head()
```

In Figure 4-4, you can see that the Energy Demand time-series dataset consists of these five columns: ID (leftmost column), timestamp, demand, precip, and temp.

Out[56]:

	timeStamp	demand	precip	temp
0	2012-01-01 00:00:00	4937.50	0.00	46.13
1	2012-01-01 01:00:00	4752.10	0.00	45.89
2	2012-01-01 02:00:00	4542.60	0.00	45.04
3	2012-01-01 03:00:00	4357.70	0.00	45.03
4	2012-01-01 04:00:00	4275.50	0.00	42.61

Figure 4-4. Exploring the Energy Demand time-series dataset

Let's do a simple plot of the data by using the following code (Figure 4-5 shows the output):

```
import matplotlib.pyplot as plt

time_column_name = 'timeStamp'
target_column_name = 'demand'

ax = plt.gca()
data.plot(kind='line',x=time_column_name,y=target_column_name,ax=ax)
plt.show()
```

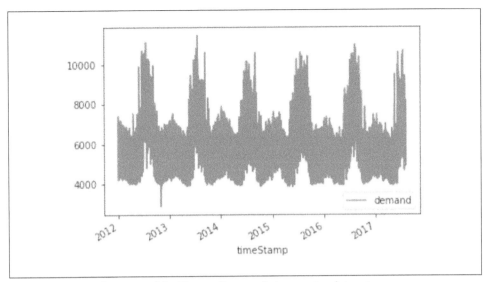

Figure 4-5. Visualization of the Energy Demand time-series dataset

Next, let's split the data into training and testing datasets, into observations before 2017-02-01 (training dataset), and observations after 2017-02-01 (testing dataset). We extract the target column (the column for the demand values) into y_train and y_test:

```
X_train = data[data[time_column_name] < '2017-02-01']
X_test = data[data[time_column_name] >= '2017-02-01']
y_train = X_train.pop(target_column_name).values
y_test = X_test.pop(target_column_name).values
```

Let's specify the automated ML configuration that we will use for forecasting. In the code that follows, notice that we specify the evaluation metrics for the AutoMLConfig object as the normalized root-mean-square error (RMSE). We also specify the Date Time column using time_column_name.

As each row of the data denotes hourly observations, it is important to specify the time horizon for prediction by using the property max_horizon. Suppose that you want to predict for the next one day (i.e., 24 hours); the value of max_horizon is set to 24. The property country_or_region is commented out in this example. This property is useful if you want to take into consideration autogenerated features that capture details about the holidays in the country specified. In this specific example, we do not need it; thus, we comment it out:

```
time_series_settings = {
    "time_column_name": time_column_name,
    "max_horizon": 24
    #"country_or_region" : 'US',
}
```

```
automl_config = AutoMLConfig(task = 'forecasting',
                    primary_metric='normalized_root_mean_squared_error',
                    iterations = 10,
                    iteration_timeout_minutes = 5,
                    X = X_train,
                    y = y_train,
                    n_cross_validations = 3,
                    path=project_folder,
                    verbosity = logging.INFO,
                    **time_series_settings)
```

Now that you have defined the `AutoMLConfig` object, you are ready to submit the experiment. Figure 4-6 presents the output of running the experiment. When the automated ML experiment is run, you will see that the experiment starts by performing auto-featurization on the time-series dataset. This is captured in the steps "Current status: DatasetFeaturization. Beginning to featurize the dataset." and "Current status: DatasetFeaturizationCompleted. Completed featurizing the dataset." After featurization is completed, model selection using automated ML begins.

```
Running on local machine
Parent Run ID: AutoML_1e023622-4df9-40ef-a4ce-0d0c0673bcc7
Current status: DatasetFeaturization. Beginning to featurize the dataset.
Current status: DatasetFeaturizationCompleted. Completed featurizing the dataset.
Current status: DatasetCrossValidationSplit. Generating CV splits.
Current status: DatasetFeaturization. Beginning to featurize the CV split.
Current status: DatasetFeaturizationCompleted. Completed featurizing the CV split.
Current status: DatasetFeaturization. Beginning to featurize the CV split.
Current status: DatasetFeaturizationCompleted. Completed featurizing the CV split.
Current status: DatasetFeaturization. Beginning to featurize the CV split.
Current status: DatasetFeaturizationCompleted. Completed featurizing the CV split.
Current status: ModelSelection. Beginning model selection.

********************************************************************************
ITERATION: The iteration being evaluated.
PIPELINE: A summary description of the pipeline being evaluated.
DURATION: Time taken for the current iteration.
METRIC: The result of computing score on the fitted pipeline.
BEST: The best observed score thus far.
********************************************************************************

 ITERATION   PIPELINE                                   DURATION    METRIC     BEST
         0   RobustScaler ElasticNet                    0:01:07     0.0796     0.0796
         1   StandardScalerWrapper ElasticNet           0:00:50     0.0945     0.0796
         2   StandardScalerWrapper ElasticNet           0:00:46     0.0812     0.0796
         3   StandardScalerWrapper RandomForest         0:00:50     0.0340     0.0340
         4   StandardScalerWrapper LightGBM             0:00:42     0.0542     0.0340
         5   StandardScalerWrapper LassoLars            0:00:41     0.0790     0.0340
         6   MinMaxScaler DecisionTree                  0:00:42     0.0319     0.0319
         7   MaxAbsScaler RandomForest                  0:00:45     0.0265     0.0265
         8   VotingEnsemble                             0:01:00     0.0249     0.0249
         9   StackEnsemble                              0:00:52     0.0178     0.0178
```

Figure 4-6. Running the automated ML experiment

During model selection, automated ML runs several iterations. Each iteration uses different data preprocessing methods (e.g., `RobustScaler`, `StandardScalerWrapper`, `MinMaxScaler`, `MaxAbsScaler`) and forecasting algorithms (`ElasticNet`, `LightGB`,

LassoLars, DecisionTree, and RandomForest). The last two iterations use different ensemble methods (e.g., VotingEnsemble and StackEnsemble). For this specific example, the best result is achieved in iteration 9, which uses StackEnsemble:

```
local_run = experiment.submit(automl_config, show_output=True)
```

Now, let's retrieve detailed information about the best run and the model. Figure 4-7 shows the summary of the engineered features. As this is a time-series dataset, you'll notice that for the feature timestamp, 11 additional features are autogenerated (i.e., EngineeredFeatureCount is shown as 11), all of data type DateTime.

```
best_run, fitted_model = local_run.get_output()

# Get the summary of the engineered features
fitted_model.named_steps['timeseriestransformer'].get_featurization_summary()
```

```
Out[68]: [{'RawFeatureName': 'precip',
           'TypeDetected': 'Numeric',
           'Dropped': 'No',
           'EngineeredFeatureCount': 2,
           'Tranformations': ['MeanImputer', 'ImputationMarker']},
          {'RawFeatureName': 'temp',
           'TypeDetected': 'Numeric',
           'Dropped': 'No',
           'EngineeredFeatureCount': 2,
           'Tranformations': ['MeanImputer', 'ImputationMarker']},
          {'RawFeatureName': 'timeStamp',
           'TypeDetected': 'DateTime',
           'Dropped': 'No',
           'EngineeredFeatureCount': 11,
           'Tranformations': ['DateTime',
           'DateTime',
           'DateTime',
           'DateTime',
           'DateTime',
           'DateTime',
           'DateTime',
           'DateTime',
           'DateTime',
           'DateTime',
           'DateTime']}]
```

Figure 4-7. Retrieving information for the best run

Let's now examine the features autogenerated for the DateTime column. To do this, we'll use fitted_model for performing forecasting, using the test data we defined earlier. From the following code, we invoke the forecast function, and the results are stored in the variables y_fcst and X_trans:

```
best_run, fitted_model = local_run.get_output()

y_query = y_test.copy().astype(np.float)
y_query.fill(np.NaN)
y_fcst, X_trans = fitted_model.forecast(X_test, y_query)
```

Next we turn to X_trans. In Figure 4-8, you can see the 11 engineered features, which took the DateTime column and divided it into the time parts (e.g., year, half, quarter, month, day, hour, am_pm, hour12, wday, qday, and week). Changing it from a Date Time to a numerical value makes it more meaningful and easier to use by the machine learning algorithms during training and scoring.

timeStamp	_automl_dummy_grain_col	precip	temp	precip_WASNULL	temp_WASNULL	year	half	quarter	month	day	hour	am_pm
2017-02-01 00:00:00	_automl_dummy_grain_col	0.00	31.45	0.00	0.00	2017	1	1	2	1	0	0
2017-02-01 01:00:00	_automl_dummy_grain_col	0.00	32.44	0.00	0.00	2017	1	1	2	1	1	0
2017-02-01 02:00:00	_automl_dummy_grain_col	0.00	33.19	0.00	0.00	2017	1	1	2	1	2	0
2017-02-01 03:00:00	_automl_dummy_grain_col	0.00	33.61	0.00	0.00	2017	1	1	2	1	3	0
2017-02-01	_automl_dummy_grain_col	0.00	32.30	0.00	0.00	2017	1	1	2	1	4	0

Figure 4-8. Engineered features for time-series forecasting

Conclusion

In this chapter, you learned about the importance of feature engineering, and how it affects the quality of the machine learning models produced. Feature engineering is an art: to do it well, it's important to understand its foundations, to receive on-the-job training, and to build your toolbox for doing feature engineering as you work through various machine learning projects. In recent years, the machine learning community has been innovating on Python libraries that enable auto-featurization. For example, you can use the Python package featuretools to perform deep feature synthesis by taking advantage of the relationships between entities, and more.

We focused in this chapter on how to use the auto-featurization capabilities provided by automated ML in the Azure Machine Learning service. Using examples of regression and forecasting, we explored how to enable auto-featurization in automated ML and how to understand the engineered features.

Though automated ML provides auto-featurization capabilities (that are continuously improving and evolving), note that it doesn't exhaustively cover all aspects of feature engineering. It's important for data scientists to perform feature engineering, taking advantage of domain expertise, before using the dataset as input to automated ML.

## CHAPTER 5

Deploying Automated Machine Learning Models

Microsoft Azure Machine Learning enables you to manage the life cycle of your machine learning models. After you have trained the models by using Azure Machine Learning's automated ML tool, you can retrieve the best model identified, and register the model with Azure Machine Learning. Model registration enables you to store varying versions of models in the machine learning workspace and makes it possible for you to easily deploy the models to different target environments.

In this chapter, we explore how to use Azure Machine Learning to do the following:

- Register the best model produced by automated ML.
- Specify and develop the scoring file. The scoring will be included as part of the container images that will be generated.
- Deploy the models to Microsoft Azure Container Instances (ACI) and Azure Kubernetes Service (AKS).
- Troubleshoot failures during model and web service deployments.

Deploying Models

In Chapter 3, you learned how to build a machine learning model using automated ML. In this section, you'll learn how to register and deploy the best model that is identified by automated ML. Azure Machine Learning supports a rich set of deployment environments, ranging from REST APIs hosted in Azure, to models deployed to different edge devices and hardware. These environments include the following:

- Azure Machine Learning Compute

- ACI
- AKS
- Azure IoT Edge

 To learn more about the up-to-date list of deployment options that are supported by Azure Machine Learning, go to the Microsoft page (*http://bit.ly/2Haqkmv*) about deploying models.

Now, let's walk through the steps that you will use to register, deploy, and test the best models that have been produced by automated ML:

1. Retrieve the best model.
2. Register the model.
3. Create the container image.
4. Deploy the model to a test environment, then test it.
5. Deploy the model to production.

Because the steps for deploying a model to the different environments are similar, we focus on deployment to ACI.

To get started with model deployment, you need one or more trained machine learning models. If you do not have a trained model yet, you can follow the steps described in the sample notebook (in this book's GitHub repository (*https://oreil.ly/Practical_Automated_ML_on_Azure*)) to train a simple regression model for predictive maintenance. The code for creating an automated ML run and submitting the experiment using an AutoMLConfig object is as follows:

```
Automl_config = AutoMLConfig(task = 'regression',
                primary_metric = 'r2_score',
                iteration_timeout_minutes = 15,
                iterations = 10,
                max_cores_per_iteration = 1,
                preprocess = False,
                experiment_exit_score = 0.985,
                X = X_train,
                y = y_train,
                X_valid = X_valid,
                y_valid = y_valid,
                debug_log = 'automl_errors.log',
                verbosity=logging.ERROR,
                path=project_folder)

# Training the predictive maintenance model using AutoML
```

```
experiment=Experiment(ws, experiment_name)
local_run = experiment.submit(Automl_config, show_output=True)
```

After the experiment has completed successfully (see Figure 5-1), you'll have access to the local_run object that you will use to register the model.

```
Running on local machine
Parent Run ID: AutoML_90386d60-b6e9-4acd-9333-0fc2d16c389d
Current status: ModelSelection. Beginning model selection.

****************************************************************************************
ITERATION: The iteration being evaluated.
PIPELINE: A summary description of the pipeline being evaluated.
DURATION: Time taken for the current iteration.
METRIC: The result of computing score on the fitted pipeline.
BEST: The best observed score thus far.
****************************************************************************************

ITERATION   PIPELINE                                         DURATION   METRIC    BEST
        0   StandardScalerWrapper LightGBM                   0:00:37    0.6113    0.6113
        1   MaxAbsScaler LightGBM                            0:00:37    0.6091    0.6113
        2   StandardScalerWrapper ExtremeRandomTrees         0:00:23    0.5328    0.6113
        3   RobustScaler LightGBM                            0:00:41    0.6114    0.6114
        4   StandardScalerWrapper LightGBM                   0:00:26    0.6282    0.6282
        5   StandardScalerWrapper LightGBM                   0:00:24    0.6293    0.6293
        6   StandardScalerWrapper ElasticNet                 0:00:19    0.5881    0.6293
        7   StandardScalerWrapper ExtremeRandomTrees         0:00:21    0.6202    0.6293
        8   VotingEnsemble                                   0:01:25    0.6434    0.6434
        9   StackEnsemble                                    0:01:51    0.6440    0.6440
```

Figure 5-1. Output from an automated ML experiment

The sample notebook for using automated ML to build and deploy the predictive maintenance model discussed in this chapter is available at *https://bit.ly/2k2e6VC*.

The predictive maintenance model uses the NASA turbofan failure dataset. More details on the dataset are available at *https://go.nasa.gov/2J6N1eK*.

Registering the Model

Before you register the trained model, you can use the get_output() function to find out more about the run that corresponds to the best-performing model. The get_out put() function returns both the best run as well as the corresponding fitted model.

What types of machine learning model can you register? You can register Python or R models using Azure Machine Learning, as well as models that have been trained using Azure Machine Learning, or pretrained models that are available externally.

Figure 5-2 shows the output from running the code block that follows. You will notice that under the hood, a *regression pipeline* is created. The regression pipeline consists of several steps: StackEnsembleRegressor, StandardScalerWrapper, and LightGBMRegressor). Notice that the number of folds for cross-validation is set to 5:

```
best_run, fitted_model = local_run.get_output()
print(best_run)
print(fitted_model)
```

```
# find the run with the highest accuracy value.
best_run, fitted_model = local_run.get_output()


executed in 9.95s, finished 11:41:44 2019-08-02


print(best_run)
executed in 40ms, finished 11:41:44 2019-08-02

Run(Experiment: automl-predictive-rul,
Id: AutoML_90386d60-b6e9-4acd-9333-0fc2d16c389d_9,
Type: None,
Status: Completed)


print(fitted_model)
executed in 216ms, finished 11:41:45 2019-08-02

RegressionPipeline(pipeline=Pipeline(memory=None,
    steps=[('stackensembleregressor', StackEnsembleRegressor(base_lea
rners=[('5', RegressionPipeline(pipeline=Pipeline(memory=None,
    steps=[('StandardScalerWrapper', <automl.client.core.common.model
_wrappers.StandardScalerWrapper object at 0x7f090ff90cf8>), ('LightGBM
Regressor', LightGBMRegressor(bo...    random_state=None, selection='cy
clic', tol=0.0001, verbose=0),
        training_cv_folds=5))]),
    stddev=None)
```

Figure 5-2. Retrieving the best run, and details of the corresponding fitted model

You are now ready to register the model. First, you specify the descriptions and tags for the model, and use the register_model() function to register the model with Azure Machine Learning. By registering the model, you are storing and versioning the model in the cloud.

Each registered model is identified by its name and version. When you register a model (with the same name) multiple times, the registry will incrementally update the version for the model stored in the registry. Metadata tags enable you to provide more information about the models that you are registering with the model registry.

You can search for the model using the metadata tags that are provided when the model is registered.

After you have registered the model, you can get the model's identifier. In the following code, you retrieve the identifier using local_run.model_id (Figure 5-3 shows the output of running the code):

```
# Register best model in workspace
description = 'AutoML-RUL-Regression-20190510'
tags = None
model = local_run.register_model(description = description, tags = tags)

print(local_run.model_id)
```

```
# register best model in workspace
description = 'AutoML-RUL-Regression-2019-01'
tags = None
model = local_run.register_model(description = description, tags = tags)

# Model_id will be used in the scoring script file
print(local_run.model_id)

executed in 18.4s, finished 11:45:14 2019-08-02

Registering model AutoML90386d60bbest
AutoML90386d60bbest
```

Figure 5-3. Getting the identifier for the model registered with Azure Machine Learning

So far, you have learned how to use the register_model() function to register a model that has been trained with Azure Machine Learning. You might have trained a model without using Azure Machine Learning or obtained a model from an external model repository (or model zoo). For example, to register the MNIST Handwritten Digit Recognition ONNX model provided in this repo (*https://oreil.ly/18z5e*), you can use Model.register() to register it by providing a local path to the model. The following code shows how to do this:

```
onnx_model_url = https://onnxzoo.blob.core.windows.net/models/opset_1/
                         mnist/mnist.tar.gz

urllib.request.urlretrieve(onnx_model_url, filename="mnist.tar.gz")
!tar xvzf mnist.tar.gz
model = Model.register(workspace = ws,
                       model_path ="mnist/model.onnx",
                       model_name = "onnx_mnist",
                       tags = {"onnx": "automl-book"},
                       description = "MNIST ONNX model",)
```

You can find out more about the Model class on Microsoft's Models documentation page (*http://bit.ly/2E2YqrW*).

Creating the Container Image

Next, we work toward deploying the model as a REST API. Azure Machine Learning helps you create the container image. The container image can be deployed to any environment where Docker is available (including Docker running on-premises). In this chapter, you'll learn how to deploy and serve the model by using either ACI or AKS.

To do this, you will need to create a scoring file (*score.py*) and the YAML file (*myenv.yml*). The scoring file is used for loading the model, making the prediction, and returning the results when the REST API is invoked. In the scoring file, you will notice that two functions need to be defined: init() and run(rawdata).

The init() function is used to load the model into a global model object. When the Docker container is started, the function is run only once. The run() function is used to predict a value based on the input data that is passed to it. Because this code is mostly used in a web service, the input that is passed via rawdata is a JSON object. The JSON object needs to be deserialized before you pass it to the model for prediction, as shown in the following code:

```
%%writefile score.py

import pickle
import json
import numpy
import azureml.train.automl
from sklearn.externals import joblib
from azureml.core.model import Model

def init():
    global model

    # This name is model.id of model that we want to deploy
    model_path = Model.get_model_path(model_name = '<<modelid>>')

    # Deserialize the model file back into a sklearn model
    model = joblib.load(model_path)

def run(input_data):
    try:
        data = json.loads(input_data)['input_data']
        data = np.array(data)
        result = model.predict(data)
```

```
        return result.tolist()
    except Exception as e:
        result = str(e)
        return json.dumps({"error": result})
```

After the code is run, the content will be written to a file called *score.py*. Figure 5-4 shows the output from running the code. We will replace the value for <<modelid>> in a later step with the actual model identifier value from local_run.model_id.

```
%%writefile score.py
import pickle
import json
import numpy as np
import azureml.train.automl
from sklearn.externals import joblib
from azureml.core.model import Model

def init():
    global model

    # this name is model.id of model that we want to deploy
    model_path = Model.get_model_path(model_name = '<<modelid>>')

    # deserialize the model file back into a sklearn model
    model = joblib.load(model_path)

def run(input_data):
    try:
        #data = json.loads(input_data)['data']
        #data = json.loads(input_data)['input_data']
        #data = np.array(data)
        result = model.predict(input_data)
        #return json.dumps({"result:result.tolist()})
        return result.tolist()
    except Exception as e:
        result = str(e)
        return json.dumps({"error": result})
executed in 280ms, finished 11:49:35 2019-08-02

Overwriting score.py
```

Figure 5-4. Creating the scoring file—score.py

After the scoring file has been created, we identify the dependencies from the run and create the YAML file, as demonstrated in the following code (Figure 5-5 shows the output from running the code):

```
experiment = Experiment(ws, experiment_name)
ml_run = AutoMLRun(experiment = experiment, run_id = local_run.id)

dependencies = ml_run.get_run_sdk_dependencies(iteration = 0)

for p in ['azureml-train-automl', 'azureml-sdk', 'azureml-core']:
    print('{}\t{}'.format(p, dependencies[p]))
```

```
experiment = Experiment(ws, experiment_name)
ml_run = AutoMLRun(experiment = experiment, run_id = local_run.id)
dependencies = ml_run.get_run_sdk_dependencies(iteration = 0)
for p in ['azureml-train-automl', 'azureml-sdk', 'azureml-core']:
    print('{}\t{}'.format(p, dependencies[p]))
```

executed in 1.69s, finished 11:50:29 2019-08-02

```
azureml-train-automl    1.0.53
azureml-sdk    1.0.53
azureml-core    1.0.53
```

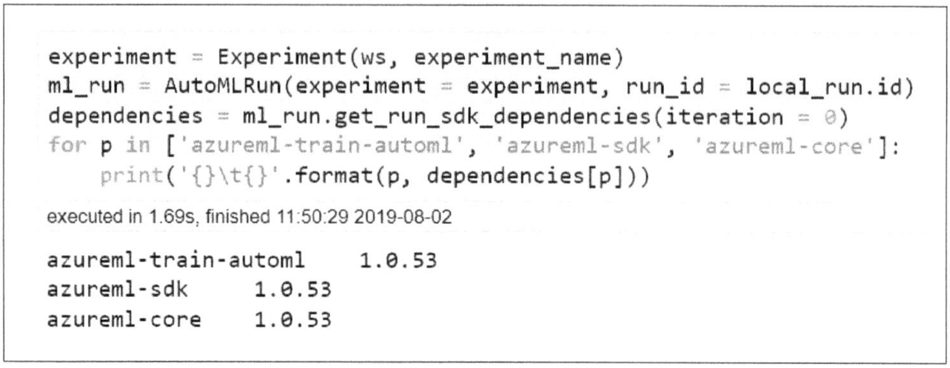

Figure 5-5. Retrieving the version of the Azure Machine Learning SDK

After you have identified the dependencies, you can create the YAML file with all of the dependencies specified by using the function CondaDependencies.create(). The function creates the environment object and enables you to serialize it to the *myenv.yml* file by using the function save_to_file(). Figure 5-6 shows the output from running the following code:

```
from azureml.core.conda_dependencies import CondaDependencies
myenv = CondaDependencies.create(conda_packages=[
                'numpy','scikit-learn','lightgbm'],
                pip_packages=['azureml-sdk[automl]'])
conda_env_file_name = 'myenv.yml'
myenv.save_to_file('.', conda_env_file_name)
```

```
from azureml.core.conda_dependencies import CondaDependencies

myenv = CondaDependencies.create(conda_packages=['numpy','scikit-learn',

conda_env_file_name = 'myenv.yml'
myenv.save_to_file('.', conda_env_file_name)
```

executed in 227ms, finished 11:51:59 2019-08-02

```
'myenv.yml'
```

Figure 5-6. Creating the environment YAML file—myenv.yml

Now that we have created both the scoring and environment YAML files, we can update the files' content with the version of the Azure Machine Learning SDK and model identifier that we obtained earlier. The following code reads the file, replaces the affected values, and writes it back to disk:

```
with open(conda_env_file_name, 'r') as cefr:
    content = cefr.read()
with open(conda_env_file_name, 'w') as cefw:
    cefw.write(content.replace(azureml.core.VERSION, dependencies['azureml-sdk']))

# Substitute the actual model id in the script file.
script_file_name = 'score.py'

with open(script_file_name, 'r') as cefr:
    content = cefr.read()
with open(script_file_name, 'w') as cefw:
    cefw.write(content.replace('<<modelid>>', local_run.model_id))
```

With the values now replaced, you're ready to configure and create the container images, which will be registered with the ACI. In the configuration of the container image, using the function `ContainerImage.image_configuration()`, you specify the runtime used, the environment file that provides the Conda dependencies, metadata tags, and a description for the container image.

When you invoke `Image.create()`, Azure Machine Learning builds the container image, and registers the container image with the ACI. Running the container creation code (from "Creating image" to "Running") usually takes several minutes. By using `image.creation.status`, you can learn whether the image creation was successful. Figure 5-7 shows the output from running the following code and verifying that the container creation is successful:

```
from azureml.core.image import Image, ContainerImage

image_config = ContainerImage.image_configuration(
                    runtime= "python",
                    execution_script = script_file_name,
                    conda_file = conda_env_file_name,
                    tags = {'area': "pred maint",
                            'type': "automl_regression"},
                    description = "Image for AutoML Predictive maintenance")
image = Image.create(name = "automlpredmaintimage",
                    models = [model],
                    image_config = image_config,
                    workspace = ws)
image.wait_for_creation(show_output = True)
if image.creation_state == 'Failed':
    print("Image build log at: " + image.image_build_log_uri)
```

```
from azureml.core.image import Image, ContainerImage

image_config = ContainerImage.image_configuration(runtime= "python",
                            execution_script = script_file_name,
                            conda_file = conda_env_file_name,
                            properties = {'secret-key': "mykey"},
                            tags = {'area': "pred maint", 'type': "automl_regression"},
                            description = "Image for automl predictive maintenance NASA")

image = Image.create(name = "automlpredmaintimage",
                        # this is the model object
                        models = [model],
                        image_config = image_config,
                        workspace = ws)

image.wait_for_creation(show_output = True)

if image.creation_state == 'Failed':
    print("Image build log at: " + image.image_build_log_uri)
```
executed in 5m 2s, finished 11:58:10 2019-08-02

```
Creating image
Running........................................................
Succeeded
Image creation operation finished for image automlpredmaintimage:48, operation "Succeeded"
```

Figure 5-7. Creating the Docker container for the predictive maintenance model

Deploying the Model for Testing

After the Docker container images have been created successfully, you are ready to deploy the model. You can deploy the container to any environment in which Docker is available (including Docker running on-premises). These include Azure Machine Learning Compute, ACI, AKS, IoT Edge, and more. Begin by deploying the Docker container to ACI for testing. For this deploy, do the following:

1. Specify the deploy configuration.
2. Deploy the Docker image to ACI.
3. Retrieve the scoring URI.

The AciWebservice class is used to specify the deploy configuration. First, we specify this for the ACI web service. In the following code, we specify a configuration that uses one CPU core with 2 GB of memory. In addition, we add metadata tags as well as a description:

```
from azureml.core.webservice import AciWebservice
aciconfig = AciWebservice.deploy_configuration(cpu_cores=1,
                memory_gb=2,
                tags={"data": "RUL",  "method" : "sklearn"},
                description='Predict RUL with Azure AutoML')
```

Next, we use the Webservice class to deploy the Docker image to the ACI. We use wait_for_deployment(True) after invoking deploy_from_image(). This requires you to wait for the completion of the web service deployment to ACI. When this is done, we print the state of the ACI web service. Figure 5-8 shows the output from running the following code:

```
from azureml.core.webservice import Webservice

aci_service_name = 'automl-book-pred-maint'
print(aci_service_name)

aci_service = Webservice.deploy_from_image(
                        deployment_config = aciconfig,
                        image = image,
                        name = aci_service_name,
                        workspace = ws)
aci_service.wait_for_deployment(True)
print(aci_service.state)
```

 The Webservice class provides various functions for deployment, including deployment from the image (what we're using here) and from the Model object, building and deploying a model locally for testing, and more. To learn how to use the various functions from the WebService class, see the Microsoft documentation page (*http://bit.ly/2VzN6i5*).

```
from azureml.core.webservice import AciWebservice

aciconfig = AciWebservice.deploy_configuration(cpu_cores=1,
                        memory_gb=1,
                        tags={"data": "RUL",  "method" : "sklearn"},
                        description='Predict RUL with Azure AutoML')
```
executed in 15ms, finished 11:58:21 2019-08-02

```
from azureml.core.webservice import Webservice

aci_service_name = 'automl-predmaint-schemainference'
print(aci_service_name)
aci_service = Webservice.deploy_from_image(deployment_config = aciconfig,
                        image = image,
                        name = aci_service_name,
                        workspace = ws)
aci_service.wait_for_deployment(True)
print(aci_service.state)
```
executed in 1m 56 0s, finished 12:00:17 2019-08-02

```
automl-predmaint-schemainference
Creating service
Running......................
SucceededACI service creation operation finished, operation "Succeeded"
Healthy
```

Figure 5-8. Deploying the web service to ACI and checking that the operation completed

Here you're learning how to use the Azure Machine Learning SDK for deploying the models created by automated ML. Azure Machine Learning supports deployment of models using the Azure CLI, via the command `az ml model deploy`. To learn how to do that, refer to this Microsoft Azure documentation page (*http:// bit.ly/2vYOGdP*).

After the ACI service deployment is complete, you will be able to use the Azure portal to see the deployment. When an ACI–based web service is created, you will notice the following:

- A deployment is created in the Azure Machine Learning workspace (see Figure 5-9).
- When an ACI instance is created for the deployment, two containers are deployed: `azureml-fe-aci` (ACI frontend for Azure Machine Learning that includes AppInsights logging), and a container (with the name that is provided during deployment) that includes the scoring code.

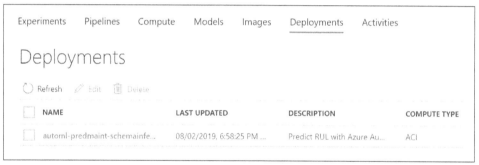

Figure 5-9. Azure portal—verifying that the deployment to ACI is complete

Using the Azure portal, you can navigate to the ACI created and click Containers. You will see the two aforementioned containers. Click the container for scoring and then click Logs. You can observe the received input and how it is processed. You can also connect to the container by clicking the Connect tab. For the Start Up Command, choose /bin/bash, and then click Connect.

If you navigate to */var/azureml-app*, you will find the files that you have been specified during deployment (e.g., *score.py*) as well as other supporting files needed for enabling the web service to be instantiated.

Once the deployment from the image is successful, you'll have a scoring URI you can use to test the deployed model:

```
print(aci_service.scoring_uri)
```

Figure 5-10 shows the scoring URI for the web service that is created.

```
print(aci_service.scoring_uri)
executed in 17ms, finished 12:03:24 2019-08-02
http://45c4e564-f58b-46ba-91f6-12e828334841.westus2.azurecontainer.io/score
```

Figure 5-10. Scoring URI for the new web service

Using the Azure portal, you can also dive deeper into the deployment log, or use the portal to connect to the container that is running. Figure 5-11 shows the deployed containers in the ACI.

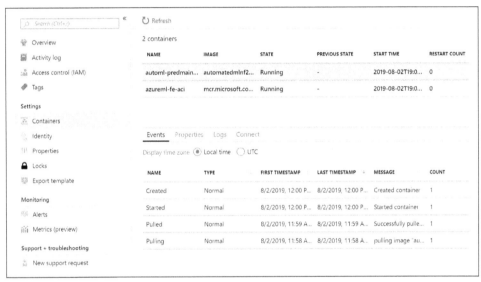

Figure 5-11. Azure portal showing the deployed container instance

Figure 5-12 shows the processes that are running in the deployed container.

Figure 5-12. Connecting to the running container

Testing a Deployed Model

With the web service deployed to ACI, you are now ready to test the web service. To do this, you randomly identify a row from X_test. X_test contains the test rows from the NASA data. You then construct the JSON payload, and perform a POST to the scoring URI, which returns the result. Figure 5-13 shows the output from running the following code:

```python
import requests
import json

# Send a random row from the test set to score
random_index = np.random.randint(0, len(X_test)-1)
X_test_row = X_test[random_index : (random_index+1)]
Y_test_row = y_test[random_index : (random_index+1)]

input_data = "{\"input_data\": " + str(X_test_row.values.tolist()) + "}"

headers = {'Content-Type':'application/json'}
resp = requests.post(aci_service.scoring_uri, input_data, headers=headers)

print("POST to url", aci_service.scoring_uri)
print("input data:", input_data)
print("label:", Y_test_row)
print("prediction:", resp.text)
```

```
    print(resp.status_code)
    print(requests.status_codes._codes[resp.status_code])
```

```
# send a random row from the test set to score
random_index = np.random.randint(0, len(X_test)-1)
X_test_row = X_test[random_index : (random_index+1)]
Y_test_row = y_test[random_index : (random_index+1)]

input_data = "{\"input_data\": " + str(X_test_row.values.tolist()) + "}"
#str(list(X_train[0].reshape(1,-1)[0])) + "}"

headers = {'Content-Type':'application/json'}

# for AKS deployment you'd need to the service key in the header as well
# api_key = service.get_key()
# headers = {'Content-Type':'application/json', 'Authorization':('Bearer '+ api_key)}

resp = requests.post(aci_service.scoring_uri, input_data, headers=headers)

print("POST to url", aci_service.scoring_uri)
print("input data:", input_data)
print("label:", Y_test_row)
print("prediction:", resp.text)
print(resp.status_code)

executed in 314ms, finished 12:06:33 2019-08-02

POST to url http://45c4e564-f58b-46ba-91f6-12e828334841.westus2.azurecontainer.io/score
input data: {"input_data": [[0.0027, 0.0002, 100.0, 518.67, 642.73, 1589.93, 1410.69, 1
4.62, 21.61, 553.62, 2388.1, 9035.59, 1.3, 47.5, 521.28, 2388.2, 8118.62, 8.4314, 0.03,
392.0, 2388.0, 100.0, 38.68, 23.2983]]}
label: [171]
prediction: [131.60946764913518]
200
```

Figure 5-13. Testing the ACI web service by using the NASA dataset

Notice in this example that we are sending a POST request directly to the scoring URI. Because the web service is backed by an ACI instance, authentication is not enabled. Deploying models to ACI is good for quickly deploying and validating your models as well as testing a model that is still in development.

Deploying to AKS

For production deployment, consider deploying the models to AKS. To do that, you will need to create an AKS cluster. You can either use the Azure CLI or Azure Machine Learning SDK to create the cluster. After you create the AKS cluster, you can use it to deploy multiple images.

Let's start by creating the AKS cluster by using the following code:

```
from azureml.core.compute import AksCompute, ComputeTarget

# Use the default configuration
# You can also customize the AKS cluster based on what you need
prov_config = AksCompute.provisioning_configuration()
```

```
aks_name = 'myaks'

# Create the cluster
aks_target = ComputeTarget.create(workspace = ws,
                    name = aks_name,
                    provisioning_configuration = prov_config)
# Wait for the AKS cluster to complete creation
aks_target.wait_for_completion(show_output = True)
```

After you've created the AKS cluster, you can deploy the model to the service. In the following code, notice that we are specifying the AKS cluster that we have created as a deployment_target:

```
from azureml.core.webservice import AksWebservice

aks_service_name = 'aks-automl-book-pred-maint'
print(aks_service_name)

aks_target = AksCompute(ws,"myaks")

aks_service = AksWebservice.deploy_from_image(image = image,
                        name = aks_service_name,
                        deployment_target = aks_target,
                        workspace = ws)

aks_service.wait_for_deployment(True)
print(aks_service.state)
```

With the model deployed to AKS, you will need to specify the service key in the header of the request before being able to invoke the scoring URI. To do that, let's modify the test scoring code that you developed earlier:

```
import requests
import json

# Send a random row from the test set to score
random_index = np.random.randint(0, len(X_test)-1)
X_test_row = X_test[random_index : (random_index+1)]
Y_test_row = y_test[random_index : (random_index+1)]

input_data = "{\"input_data\": " + str(X_test_row.values.tolist()) + "}"

# For AKS deployment you need the service key in the header as well
headers = {'Content-Type':'application/json'}
api_key = aks_service.get_keys()[0]
headers = {'Content-Type':'application/json',
                        'Authorization':('Bearer '+ api_key)}

resp = requests.post(aks_service.scoring_uri, input_data, headers=headers)

print("POST to url", aks_service.scoring_uri)
print("input data:", input_data)
print("label:", Y_test_row)
```

```
print("prediction:", resp.text)
print(resp.status_code)
```

Swagger Documentation for the Web Service

After you have deployed the machine learning web service to various compute environments, it is important to provide good documentation describing how to use the APIs. This helps to accelerate development of applications that depend on the APIs for prediction. Because the machine learning APIs that you need to manage will evolve over time (especially during development), it is important to keep the documentation up-to-date.

Swagger is an open source software framework that is used by many developers who are designing, developing, and documenting RESTful web services. Swagger documentation makes it easy for a developer to quickly describe and document the inputs and outputs of a web service. Swagger documentation has evolved over the years to become a common way of describing RESTful APIs. Having autogenerated Swagger documentation helps to ensure that up-to-date information is always available when you deploy your machine learning model and make it available as a web service.

When you deploy a model using Azure Machine Learning, you can use the Python inference-schema package when creating the scoring file. The inference-schema package allows you to add function decorators that enable Swagger documentation to be generated as well as enforce the schema types.

First, import the relevant classes from the inference-schema package, as follows:

```
from inference_schema.schema_decorators import input_schema, output_schema
from inference_schema.parameter_types.numpy_parameter_type import
                          NumpyParameterType
```

After you have imported the various classes, you can specify the input and output schema, by providing the input_schema and output_schema as decorators for the run() function. The sample input and output data is provided as part of the input_sample and output_sample variables:

```
@input_schema('input_data', NumpyParameterType(input_sample))
@output_schema(NumpyParameterType(output_sample))
```

The following code shows the *score.py* file, with the decorators specified:

```
%%writefile score.py
import pickle
import json
import numpy as np
from sklearn.externals import joblib

import azureml.train.automl
from azureml.core.model import Model
```

```
from inference_schema.schema_decorators import input_schema, output_schema
from inference_schema.parameter_types.numpy_parameter_type
                                         import NumpyParameterType

def init():
    global model

    # Identifier for the model (model.id) to be deployed
    model_path = Model.get_model_path(model_name = '<<modelid>>')

    # Deserialize the model file back into a sklearn model
    model = joblib.load(model_path)
X_test_row = np.array([[-0.0006, -0.0004, 100.0, 518.67,
                642.25, 1589.25, 1412.42, 14.62, 21.61, 553.88,
                2388.15, 9043.21, 1.3, 47.45, 521.88, 2388.18,
                8131.61, 8.4807, 0.03, 392.0, 2388.0,
                100.0, 38.6, 23.2946]])

input_sample = X_test_row
output_sample = np.array([120.0])


@input_schema('input_data', NumpyParameterType(input_sample))
@output_schema(NumpyParameterType(output_sample))
def run(input_data):

    try:
        result = model.predict(input_data)
        return result.tolist()

    except Exception as e:
        result = str(e)
        return json.dumps({"error": result})
```

After you have the *score.py* file defined and the model deployed, you can retrieve the Swagger using the Swagger URI, using `print(aci_service.swagger_uri)`.

This enables you to download the file *swagger.json*, which contains the Swagger documentation for the API. For an example of the *swagger.json* generated, visit this book's GitHub repository (*http://bit.ly/30gu2nz*). You can also generate the documentation by importing the API using SwaggerHub (*https://oreil.ly/M818e*).

Debugging a Deployment

As you work toward deploying your machine learning models to various compute environments (e.g., ACI, AKS), you might encounter situations in which the deployment fails (e.g., container terminated) or the scoring API is not returning the results you are expecting. In this section, we cover some common deployment failures and show you how to resolve them.

Web Service Deployment Fails

After a container image is created and you deploy the image using `Webser vice.deploy_from_image()`, the ACI deployment might fail and the web service will not be available. As a result, you might see the following error message:

```
[test]

FailedACI service creation operation finished, operation "Failed"
Service creation polling reached terminal state, current service state: Failed
{
  "code": "AciDeploymentFailed",
  "message": "Aci Deployment failed with exception: Your container application
  crashed. This may be caused by errors in your scoring file's init() function.
  Please check the logs for your container instance automl-book-pred-maint2.
  You can also try to run image
  automatedmlnf2e4863f.azurecr.io/automlpredmaintimage-bug:1 locally.
  Please refer to http://aka.ms/debugimage for more information.",
  "details": [
    {
      "code": "CrashLoopBackOff",
      "message": "Your container application crashed. This may be caused by
      errors in your scoring file's init() function.
      \nPlease check the logs for your container instance
                                              automl-book-pred-maint2.
      \nYou can also try to run image
      automatedmlnf2e4863f.azurecr.io/automlpredmaintimage-bug:1 locally.
      Please refer to http://aka.ms/debugimage for more information."
    }
  ]
}
Failed
```

To debug what caused the service creation to fail, download the container image using the URI provided in the error message. At the same time, you can use the Azure portal to investigate. Navigate to the resource group where the Azure Machine Learning workspace has been created, and find the ACI that corresponds to the service you're creating. Figure 5-14 shows an example of the ACI. To investigate, do the following:

1. In the pane on the left, click Containers.

Figure 5-14. The container instance (automl-book-pred-maint2) to which the container image is deployed

2. Click the container that displays the state as Waiting, and the previous state as Terminated, as shown in Figure 5-15.

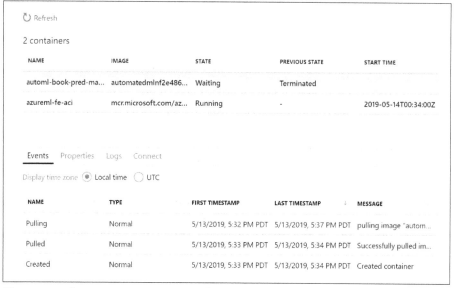

Figure 5-15. Investigating a terminated container in ACI

3. Click the Logs tab, and you will see the logs and the errors causing the container to fail to boot, as depicted in Figure 5-16.

```
   import create_app
File "/var/azureml-app/create_app.py", line 4, in <module>
   from app import main
File "/var/azureml-app/app.py", line 13, in <module>
   import main as user_main
File "/var/azureml-app/main.py", line 17, in <module>
   driver_module_spec.loader.exec_module(driver_module)
File "score.py", line 31
   data = np.array(data)
        ^
SyntaxError: invalid syntax
Worker exiting (pid: 45)
Shutting down: Master
Reason: Worker failed to boot.
2019-05-14T00:39:59,577894773+00:00 - gunicorn/finish 3 0
2019-05-14T00:39:59,578925788+00:00 - Exit code 3 is not normal. Killing image.
```

Figure 5-16. Error causing the container to fail to start

To learn how to troubleshoot Azure Machine Learning AKS and
ACI deployments, see this Microsoft documentation page on the
topic (*http://bit.ly/2VyQtFZ*).

Conclusion

In this chapter, you learned how to register, deploy, and test the models produced by
automated ML to ACI. You also learned how to specify the input and output schema
for the web service so that you can generate Swagger documentation. Sometimes you
might have a buggy scoring script that causes deployment to fail, and containers
might fail to start. For these circumstances, you learned how to use the Azure portal
as well as the Azure Machine Learning Python SDK to debug a failed deployment.

## CHAPTER 6

Classification and Regression

A key ingredient for successful machine learning implementations (based on discussions with many data scientists, machine learning engineers, and product managers) is being able to map the business problem and the desired outcome to the appropriate machine learning problem (or having a frank conversation that machine learning will not solve the problem!). *Classification* and *regression* are two common machine learning techniques that are used.

In this chapter, we cover the basics of classification and regression and show you how to map a business use case to a classification or regression problem. You'll learn how to use Microsoft Azure Machine Learning—specifically, automated ML—to automatically select the best classification or regression models for your specific use case.

Need to Get Started with Azure Machine Learning?

If you're getting started with Azure Machine Learning, refer to Chapter 3 to understand the basic concepts before diving into this chapter.

What Is Classification and Regression?

In supervised learning, you have a set of independent features, X, and a target feature, Y. The machine learning task is to map from X → Y. Both classification and regression are supervised learning, with a requirement on the availability of labeled data.

To train a high-quality model that performs well for testing data and for generalizing new unseen data, examples need to be sufficiently representative of the test data. One underlying assumption for many supervised learning algorithms is that the data distribution of training examples is identical to that of the test examples (including unseen examples).

In many real-world problems, this is often untrue. Either your data has very few objects with the target feature that you want to predict (known as the *class imbalance*, or the *minority class problem*), or it isn't of good quality. In some situations, you might not even have labeled data! Over the years, the machine learning community has invented clever ways to deal with each of these problems (e.g., using the Synthetic Minority Oversampling Technique, or SMOTE, to deal with class imbalance), but it's beyond the scope of this book to go into detail about them.

When Y is a discrete feature, and you're trying to predict the class/label, you are dealing with a *classification* problem. Classification helps predict which category (or class) an object belongs to. When classification is used for data with two distinct classes, we often refer to it as *binary classification*. If there are more than two distinct classes, it is a *multiclass classification* problem. For example, predicting whether a person is a good or bad credit risk is a binary classification problem (because there are two distinct classes: good or bad). Predicting a book category (e.g., fairytale, cookbook, biography, travel, and so on) is a multiclass classification problem.

When Y is a continuous feature that you are trying to predict, you are dealing with a *regression* problem. Regression helps to predict a continuous value. For example, in manufacturing's predictive maintenance scenarios, regression models are used to predict the lifespan for systems and equipment. In health care, regression is used to predict health-care costs, length of hospital stays for patients, and more. Figure 6-1 shows a typical data science process for training and evaluating machine learning models. The same workflow applies to both classification and regression problems.

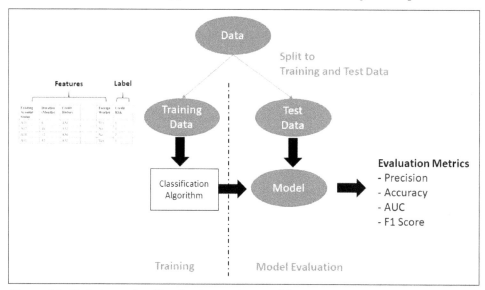

Figure 6-1. Training a classification/regression model

Data is first split into training and testing data. The training data is used as inputs to a classification/regression algorithm. A machine learning model is produced once training completes, after which it's The evaluated using the test data. As part of model evaluation, you'll compute different types of metrics (e.g., precision, accuracy, AUC, F1-score, and so on), which helps you determine its quality.

Let's illustrate this with an example on credit-risk scoring. In financial services, credit-risk scoring enables a bank to make credit decisions for customers. The German Credit Risk dataset consists of 1,000 rows (Table 6-1 shows a subset of the dataset). Each row uses a set of features (or attributes, or properties) to describe a person. The last column is the class/label (i.e., Credit Risk), which provides information on whether the person is a credit risk.

 The German Credit Risk dataset is available in the UCI Machine Learning Repository (*http://bit.ly/2CxvDet*). The dataset was contributed to the machine learning community in 1994 by Professor Hans Hofmann and consists of 20 features (7 numerical, 13 categorical), and one credit risk label.

Download the file *german.data* from the UCI Machine Learning Repository:

```
import pandas as pd
columns = ['status_checking_acc', 'duration_months', 'credit_history',
    'purpose', 'credit_amount', 'saving_acc_bonds',
    'present_emp_since','installment_rate', 'personal_status',
    'other_debtors', 'residing_since', 'property', 'age_years',
    'inst_plans', 'housing', 'num_existing_credits', 'job',
    'dependents', 'telephone', 'foreign_worker', 'status']

creditg_df = pd.read_csv(
    'https://archive.ics.uci.edu/ml/machine-learning-databases/statlog
                        /german/german.data',
delim_whitespace = True, header = None )
# Assign the header row to
creditg_df.columns = columns

# Get the initial rows of data
creditg_df.head()
```

After you download the data, observe that in each row, the first few columns (e.g., existing account status, duration, credit history, foreign worker) describe different personal attributes. In Table 6-1, you can see that the first column shows the account status for the person's checking account. A11 through A13 denote the amount available in the checking account (amounts are in DM, Deutsche Marks, the German currency until 2002). A14 indicates that the person has no checking account. For illustration purposes, we omitted many features. The last column shows the credit risk: a value of 1 indicates no credit risk, and 2 indicates a credit risk.

Table 6-1. German Credit Risk dataset

Existing account status	Duration (months)	Credit history	...	Foreign worker	Credit risk
A11	6	A34	...	Yes	1
A12	48	A32	...	No	1
A14	12	A34	...	No	2
A11	42	A32	...	Yes	1

Before we dive deeper into the German Credit Risk dataset, let's review classification and regression algorithms.

Classification and Regression Algorithms

A rich set of classification and regression algorithms has been developed over the years by the machine learning community. Commonly used classification algorithms include the naïve Bayes classifier, support vector machines (SVMs), *k*-nearest neighbor, decision tree, and random forest. For regression, decision trees, elastic nets, LARS Lasso, stochastic gradient descent (SGD), and SVMs, are commonly used.

If you're asking which classification/regression algorithm should I be using?, the answer is: it depends. Often, a data scientist tries different algorithms (depending on the problem, the dataset size, requirements for explainable models, speed of the algorithms, and more). The trade-off is often between speed, model evaluation metrics (e.g., accuracy), and explainable results.

For example, if you're looking at the computational speed at which the initial solution arrives, you might consider decision trees (or any tree-based variant) or simple linear regression approaches. However, if you're optimizing for accuracy (and other metrics), you might use random forests, SVMs, or gradient boosting trees. Often, the best result is an ensemble of different classification/regression models.

For a deeper dive into how each classification algorithm works, refer to Professor Tom Mitchell's Machine Learning course (*http://bit.ly/2Tqiqtx*), which provides a fantastic discussion on the different machine learning algorithms.

New to machine learning? Refer to this Microsoft cheat sheet (*http://bit.ly/2YhnjJ2*) for the different classification algorithms and the use cases in which they can be applied.

Figure 6-2 shows an example of a possible decision tree that is trained using the German Credit Risk dataset. You will notice that the tree starts with a split attribute–account status. If the values for account status are A13, A14, the person doesn't present a credit risk. The tree further chooses other split attributes (duration and credit history) and uses this to further determine whether a person is a credit risk.

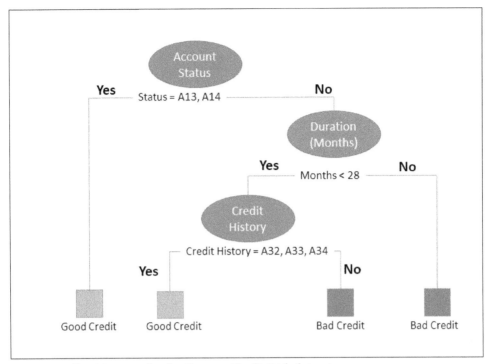

Figure 6-2. Decision tree for the German Credit Risk dataset

Each of these classification algorithms has hyperparameters that need to be tuned. Also, the data distribution, dimensionality of data, sparseness of data, and whether the data is linearly separable matter. As data scientists mature in their practice, they build their toolboxes and knowledge of the algorithms to use (based on familiarity with how the algorithms work, and how to tune the hyperparameters).

If you are interested in experimenting with different classification algorithms and datasets, scikit-learn provides a rich library of various classification algorithms and is a good Python machine learning library to get started with.

Using Automated ML for Classification and Regression

Let's begin to get our hands dirty with a classification problem. To jumpstart your learning of using automated ML for classification of credit risks using the German Credit Risk dataset, you can use the notebook provided on GitHub and run them using Microsoft Azure Notebooks (*https://notebooks.azure.com/*).

Though automated ML seems almost magical (i.e., given a dataset, perform some auto feature engineering, enumerate through different types of models, and select the best model), having the right input data will help significantly improve the quality of the models.

The sample notebook for using automated ML with Azure Machine Learning to train a credit risk model is available at *https://bit.ly/2m3xlyP*.

A rich set of classification and regression algorithms is supported when using automated ML, as shown in Table 6-2.

Table 6-2. Classification and regression algorithms supported by automated ML in Azure Machine Learning

Type of algorithm	Classification	Regression
C-SVC	✓	
Decision tree	✓	✓
Elastic net		✓
Extremely randomized trees	✓	✓
Gradient boosting	✓	✓
k-nearest neighbors	✓	✓
LARS Lasso		✓
Light GBM	✓	✓
Linear SVC	✓	
Logistic regression	✓	
Naïve Bayes	✓	
Random forest	✓	✓
SGD	✓	✓

To get the updated list of classification algorithms supported by automated ML, and to understand details about how each algorithm works, refer to this Microsoft documentation (*http://bit.ly/2TXdUYN*).

Setting up the Azure Machine Learning workspace

Previously, you learned how to set up your Azure Machine Learning workspace and prepared the configuration file with the subscription ID, resource group, and workspace name. Use the following code to set up that configuration file:

```
config.json
{
    "subscription_id": "<Replace with Azure Subscription ID>",
    "resource_group": "oreillybook",
    "workspace_name": "automl-tutorials"
}
```

When using Azure Notebooks, the *config.json* file should be stored in the same folder or in the *aml_config* folder, as shown in Figure 6-3.

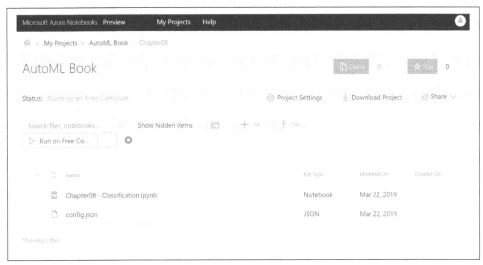

Figure 6-3. Getting started with running Azure Notebooks

After you've uploaded these files to Azure Notebooks or your own local Jupyter Notebook environment, you are ready to get started. Let's begin by importing the relevant Python packages that you will use in this exercise:

```
import numpy as np
import pandas as pd
from sklearn.model_selection import train_test_split
import logging
```

Next, import the Azure Machine Learning SDK (`azureml-sdk`):

```
import azureml.core
from azureml.core.experiment import Experiment
from azureml.core.workspace import Workspace
from azureml.train.automl import AutoMLConfig
```

After you've imported the relevant Python packages, you will create the Azure Machine Learning workspace using the values from *config.json*.

`Workspace.from_config()` reads the *config.json* file, which is either stored in either the same folder as the notebook or *aml_config/config.json*. As discussed in earlier chapters, the workspace object stores information about the Azure subscription, and information about various resources used. After you create it, it also creates a cloud resource that monitors and tracks the model runs:

```
ws = Workspace.from_config()

# Populate a workspace info object
```

```
workspace_info = {}
workspace_info['SDK version'] = azureml.core.VERSION
workspace_info['Subscription ID'] = ws.subscription_id
workspace_info['Workspace Name'] = ws.name
workspace_info['Resource Group'] = ws.resource_group
workspace_info['Location'] = ws.location
pd.set_option('display.max_colwidth', -1)
workspace_info = pd.DataFrame(data = workspace_info, index = [''])
workspace_info.T
```

After you run the Python code, you will see the output shown in Figure 6-4, which provides information about the version of the Azure Machine Learning SDK, the Azure subscription ID, and the name and location of the Azure Machine Learning workspace that's been created.

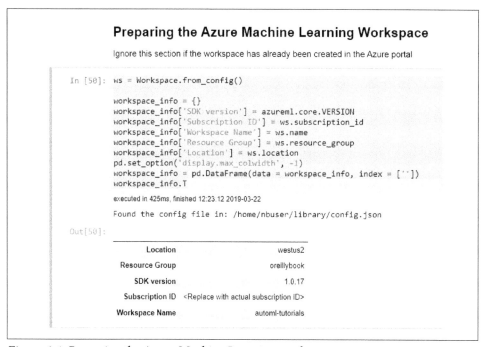

Figure 6-4. Preparing the Azure Machine Learning workspace

If this is the first time you are running the code in Azure Notebooks, you might see the following warning message:

```
Warning: Falling back to use azure cli login credentials. If you run your
code in unattended mode, i.e., where you can't give a user input, then
we recommend to use ServicePrincipalAuthentication or MsiAuthentication.

Found the config file in: /home/nbuser/library/config.json Performing
interactive authentication. Please follow the instructions on the terminal.
```

```
To sign in, use a web browser to open the page https://microsoft.com/devicelogin
and enter the code &lt;9-digit code&gt; to authenticate.
```

To authenticate with Azure, click *https://microsoft.com/devicelogin* and enter the authentication code that is provided. After you have logged in using a valid credential, you can rerun the cell, and you will be authenticated.

To run the code as part of an unattended operation, you'll need to set up an Azure Service Principal and use that to log in programmatically. To learn more about how to authenticate with Azure Machine Learning, visit this GitHub repository (*http://bit.ly/2CEBxdM*).

Next, after you've created the Azure Machine Learning workspace, you need to create the experiment object that will be used for this exercise. In the code that follows, notice that we pass the reference to the workspace object that we created earlier when creating the experiment. We also specify a project folder to contain the list of files that will be created, as shown in Figure 6-5.

```
# Choose the experiment name and specify the project folder.

experiment_name = 'automl-classification'
project_folder = './book/automl-classification'

experiment = Experiment(ws, experiment_name)
```

```
In [17]:   # Choose a name for the experiment and specify the project folder.
           experiment_name = 'automl-classification'
           project_folder = './book/automl-classification'

           experiment = Experiment(ws, experiment_name)

           executed in 4ms, finished 11:54:31 2019-03-22
```

Figure 6-5. Creating the experiment and specifying the project folder

Data preparation

For this exercise, we're using data from the UCI Machine Learning Repository (*http://bit.ly/2Opc38V*), which contains a rich collection of datasets for both classification and regression problems. Another good repository of open machine learning datasets is OpenML.org (*http://bit.ly/2HGjHLE*). The German Credit Risk dataset is available in both dataset repositories.

Because the *german.data* file from the UCI Machine Learning Repository does not contain a header row, we first define the names of each of the columns. This helps us reference the column names as we work with the dataset. After the following code is executed, you'll see the first five rows of the dataset shown in Figure 6-6, in which each row has 21 columns, with the last column being the label column, named Status:

```
# Define the column
columns = ['status_checking_acc', 'duration_months', 'credit_history',
           'purpose', 'credit_amount','saving_acc_bonds',
           'present_emp_since', 'installment_rate','personal_status',
           'other_debtors', 'residing_since', 'property',
           'age_years','inst_plans', 'housing', 'num_existing_credits',
           'job', 'dependents', 'telephone', 'foreign_worker', 'status']

creditg_df = pd.read_csv(
           'https://archive.ics.uci.edu/ml/
    machine-learning-databases/statlog/german/german.data',
    delim_whitespace = True, header = None )
creditg_df.columns = columns
creditg_df.head()
```

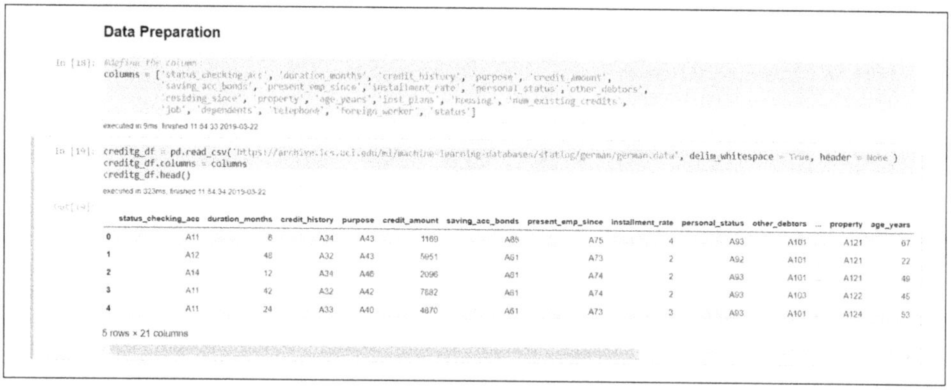

Figure 6-6. Specifying the name of the columns and loading the data

The Status column is the class that we are trying to build a model for predicting. Let's look at the number of unique values for the Status column. The values in the status column are 1 and 2; 1 denotes good credit, and 2 denotes bad credit. To make it easier to read, we subtract 1 from the values so that we use a value of 0 to represent good credit, and 1 to represent that the person has bad credit:

```
# Get the unique values in the Status Column
creditg_df.status = creditg_df.status - 1
creditg_df['status'].unique()
```

In addition, we also separated out the column with the target feature:

```
# Get the label column, and remove the label column from the dataframe
# When axis is 1, columns specified are dropped

target = creditg_df["status"]
creditg_df = creditg_df.drop(labels='status',axis=1)
```

We are now ready to split the data into train and test data. In this exercise, we do a 70/30 split (i.e., 70% of the data for training, and the remainder for testing). In the following code, you can see that we pass in the reference for the target column, as well, when we call train_test_split:

```
# Split into train and test data
X_train, X_test, y_train, y_test =
    train_test_split(creditg_df, target, test_size=0.3)

# Convert y_train and y_test from Pandas Series to ndArray
y_train = y_train.values
y_test = y_test.values
```

After you have split the data into train and test data, you should double-check both DataFrames—X_train and X_test.

Both DataFrames should have 20 columns, as shown in Figure 6-7. Because train_test_split returns the training and testing label columns as Pandas Series (denoted by y_train, and y_test), we can convert both of these objects to either ndArray or DataFrame. This will be used as one of the inputs to the AutoMLConfig object that will be created.

```
In [57]: # Understand the variables
         X_test.info()

         executed in 17ms, finished 14:38:02 2019-03-25

         <class 'pandas.core.frame.DataFrame'>
         Int64Index: 300 entries, 864 to 741
         Data columns (total 20 columns):
         status_checking_acc     300 non-null object
         duration_months         300 non-null int64
         credit_history          300 non-null object
         purpose                 300 non-null object
         credit_amount           300 non-null int64
         saving_acc_bonds        300 non-null object
         present_emp_since        300 non-null object
         installment_rate        300 non-null int64
         personal_status         300 non-null object
         other_debtors           300 non-null object
         residing_since          300 non-null int64
         property                300 non-null object
         age_years               300 non-null int64
         inst_plans              300 non-null object
         housing                 300 non-null object
         num_existing_credits    300 non-null int64
         job                     300 non-null object
         dependents              300 non-null int64
         telephone               300 non-null object
         foreign_worker          300 non-null object
         dtypes: int64(7), object(13)
         memory usage: 49.2+ KB
```

Figure 6-7. Information about DataFrame X_test

Using automated ML to train the model

We are ready to use automated ML to train the classification model for the German Credit Risk problem.

But before we do that, let's look at the metrics available for tuning when using automated ML, by using the function `get_primary_metrics()`. Figure 6-8 shows the output. You'll see that the common classification metrics are supported. These include accuracy, precision, AUC, and the weighted precision scores:

```
# Explore the metrics that are available for classification
azureml.train.automl.utilities.get_primary_metrics('classification')
```

```
In [16]:  # Explore the metrics that are available for classification
          azureml.train.automl.utilities.get_primary_metrics('classification')

          executed in 18ms, finished 14:54:31 2019-03-25

Out[16]:  ['average_precision_score_weighted',
           'norm_macro_recall',
           'AUC_weighted',
           'accuracy',
           'precision_score_weighted']
```

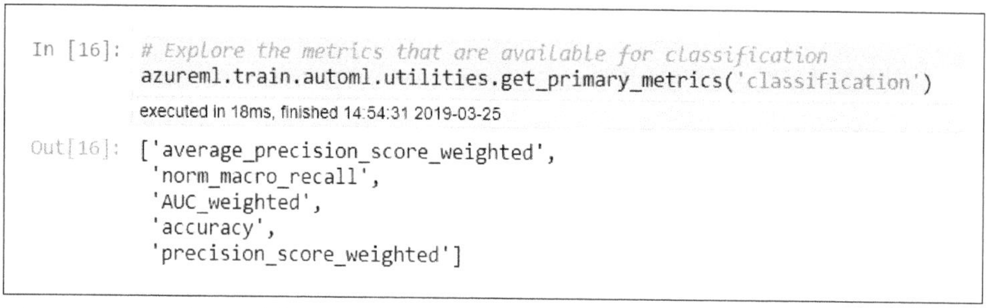

Figure 6-8. Metrics used for classification models

Let's define the common automated ML settings used in multiple experiments:

```
import time
automl_settings = {
    "name": "AutoML_Book_CH08_Classification_{0}".format(time.time()),
    "iteration_timeout_minutes": 10,
    "iterations": 30,
    "primary_metric": 'AUC_weighted',
    "preprocess": True,
    "max_concurrent_iterations": 10,
    "verbosity": logging.INFO
}
```

Next, we create the `AutoMLConfig` object that specifies the automated ML settings and the training data (including the label column `y_train`). We specify the number of cross-validations to be performed as 5:

```
automl_config = AutoMLConfig(
                    task = 'classification',
                    debug_log = 'automl_errors.log',
                    X = X_train,
                    y = y_train,
                    n_cross_validations = 5,
                    path = project_folder,
                    **automl_settings
                )
```

When creating the `AutoMLConfig` object, you will notice that in this example, we specify the task as `classification`. If you are using automated ML for automatically selecting the best regression models, you should specify the task as `regression`.

To find out about the various knobs that you can use when creating the `AutoMLConfig` object, refer to *https://bit.ly/2lZWXwo*. You can use `whitelist_models` to specify a list of algorithms to be used when searching for the best model with automated ML. You can also specify the list of models that are ignored in the experiment iteration by using `blacklist_models`.

After you've created the `AutoMLConfig` object, you are ready to submit the experiment, as follows:

```
local_run = experiment.submit(automl_config, show_output = True)
```

When the experiment has been submitted, automated ML will run and evaluate several iterations. Each iteration will use different classification algorithms as well as auto-featurization techniques, and show you the evaluation metrics. The best iteration score will also be shown. Figure 6-9 shows the output from the 30 iterations that are evaluated.

Notice that iteration 14, which uses logistic regression, achieved the best model score of 0.7727 initially. And in iteration 30 (the last one), an ensemble was used, which improved the best model score from 0.7727 to 0.7916. You will also see the explanation for each column shown in the experiment output (e.g., SAMPLING %, DURATION, METRIC, BEST).

When the experiment has completed successfully, you can view the details of the run in the Azure portal:

```
local_run
```

Or by using the automated ML Jupyter Notebook widgets:

```
import azureml.widgets
from azureml.widgets import RunDetails
RunDetails(local_run).show()
```

 If you have not installed the Python package for the widget, you can also pip install `azureml-widgets`.

```
In [21]:  local_run = experiment.submit(automl_config, show_output = True)
```

executed in 11m 59s, finished 15:17:11 2019-03-25

```
Running on local machine
Parent Run ID: AutoML_37e1a0dc-e7ea-4d87-b7c3-d59e00d5b129
********************************************************************************************
ITERATION: The iteration being evaluated.
PIPELINE: A summary description of the pipeline being evaluated.
SAMPLING %: Percent of the training data to sample.
DURATION: Time taken for the current iteration.
METRIC: The result of computing score on the fitted pipeline.
BEST: The best observed score thus far.
********************************************************************************************
```

ITERATION	PIPELINE	SAMPLING %	DURATION	METRIC	BEST
0	MaxAbsScaler LightGBM	100.0000	0:00:28	0.7699	0.7699
1	MaxAbsScaler LightGBM	100.0000	0:00:21	0.7537	0.7699
2	MaxAbsScaler LightGBM	100.0000	0:00:20	0.7724	0.7724
3	StandardScalerWrapper LightGBM	100.0000	0:00:19	0.7705	0.7724
4	MaxAbsScaler LogisticRegression	100.0000	0:00:21	0.7668	0.7724
5	StandardScalerWrapper LightGBM	100.0000	0:00:19	0.7521	0.7724
6	MaxAbsScaler LightGBM	100.0000	0:00:21	0.7663	0.7724
7	MaxAbsScaler LightGBM	100.0000	0:00:19	0.7623	0.7724
8	SparseNormalizer LightGBM	100.0000	0:00:19	0.7608	0.7724
9	StandardScalerWrapper LightGBM	100.0000	0:00:22	0.7435	0.7724
10	StandardScalerWrapper LightGBM	100.0000	0:00:21	0.7715	0.7724
11	SparseNormalizer LightGBM	100.0000	0:00:20	0.7296	0.7724
12	TruncatedSVDWrapper LightGBM	100.0000	0:00:29	0.7523	0.7724
13	MaxAbsScaler LightGBM	100.0000	0:00:23	0.7615	0.7724
14	MaxAbsScaler LogisticRegression	100.0000	0:00:21	0.7727	0.7727
15	MaxAbsScaler LightGBM	100.0000	0:00:21	0.7424	0.7727
16	MaxAbsScaler LightGBM	100.0000	0:00:20	0.7647	0.7727
17	MaxAbsScaler LightGBM	100.0000	0:00:20	0.7648	0.7727
18	StandardScalerWrapper LightGBM	100.0000	0:00:18	0.7648	0.7727
19	StandardScalerWrapper LightGBM	100.0000	0:00:19	0.7701	0.7727
20	MaxAbsScaler LogisticRegression	100.0000	0:00:22	0.7572	0.7727
21	MaxAbsScaler LightGBM	100.0000	0:00:23	0.7647	0.7727
22	MaxAbsScaler LightGBM	100.0000	0:00:22	0.7549	0.7727
23	MaxAbsScaler LightGBM	100.0000	0:00:24	0.7593	0.7727
24	MaxAbsScaler LightGBM	100.0000	0:00:20	0.7619	0.7727
25	StandardScalerWrapper LogisticRegression	100.0000	0:00:25	0.7543	0.7727
26	MaxAbsScaler LogisticRegression	100.0000	0:00:22	0.7635	0.7727
27	StandardScalerWrapper GradientBoosting	100.0000	0:00:22	0.7707	0.7727
28	MaxAbsScaler ExtremeRandomTrees	100.0000	0:00:25	0.6979	0.7727
29	Ensemble	100.0000	0:01:06	0.7916	0.7916

Figure 6-9. Output from submitting the automated ML classification experiment

As shown in Figure 6-10, if you click Link to Azure Portal, you will see the details from the latest run that you have completed. You can also deep dive into the logs that are created from running the experiments.

```
In [22]:  local_run
```

executed in 549ms, finished 15:24:02 2019-03-25

Out[22]:

Experiment	Id	Type	Status	Details Page	Docs Page
automl-classification	AutoML_37e1a0dc-e7ea-4d87-b7c3-d59e00d5b129	automl	Completed	Link to Azure Portal	Link to Documentation

Figure 6-10. Getting information about local_run

Figure 6-11 shows the details for the run, with run number 347. From the chart, you can see the performance of a model in each iteration of the run.

Figure 6-11. Azure portal—details for a run of an experiment

Once you install the widgets, you're ready to see the run details directly in Azure Notebooks.

Figure 6-12 shows the output from RunDetails(local_run).show(). You can also click each iteration to view more details. For example, if you click the last iteration (shown as the first row) for Ensemble, you will see detailed charts that capture the precision-recall, multiclass ROC, lift curve, gains curve, and calibration curve for the iteration. The confusion matrix is also shown.

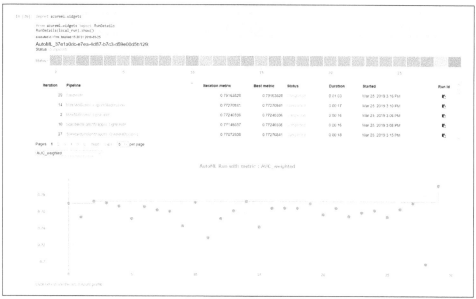

Figure 6-12. Using automated ML Jupyter Notebook widgets

A subset of this view is shown in Figure 6-13.

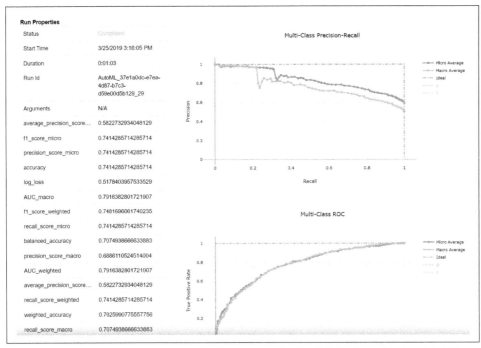

Figure 6-13. Using the automated ML Jupyter Notebook widgets to understand details about the run

Instead of interactively clicking each iteration, you can tabulate the metrics for each iteration in a run by using `get_children()` (the output is shown in Figure 6-14):

```
# Get all child runs
children = list(local_run.get_children())
metricslist = {}
for run in children:
    properties = run.get_properties()
    metrics = {k: v for k,
        v in run.get_metrics().items() if isinstance(v, float)}
    metricslist[int(properties['iteration'])] = metrics
rundata = pd.DataFrame(metricslist).sort_index(1)
rundata
```

```
In [28]:  # Get all child runs
          children = list(local_run.get_children())
          metricslist = {}
          for run in children:
              properties = run.get_properties()
              metrics = {k: v for k, v in run.get_metrics().items() if isinstance(v, float)}
              metricslist[int(properties['iteration'])] = metrics

          rundata = pd.DataFrame(metricslist).sort_index(1)
          rundata
          executed in 19.8s, finished 15:44:54 2019-03-25
```

Out[28]:

	0	1	2	3	4	5	6	7	8	9	...	20	21	22	23	24	25	26	27	28	29
AUC_macro	0.77	0.75	0.77	0.77	0.77	0.75	0.77	0.76	0.76	0.74	...	0.76	0.76	0.75	0.76	0.76	0.75	0.76	0.77	0.70	0.79
AUC_micro	0.77	0.75	0.77	0.77	0.77	0.75	0.77	0.76	0.76	0.74	.	0.76	0.76	0.75	0.76	0.76	0.75	0.76	0.77	0.70	0.79
AUC_weighted	0.77	0.75	0.77	0.77	0.77	0.75	0.77	0.76	0.76	0.74	...	0.76	0.76	0.75	0.76	0.76	0.75	0.76	0.77	0.70	0.79
accuracy	0.73	0.74	0.75	0.75	0.71	0.73	0.74	0.75	0.74	0.72	..	0.71	0.74	0.75	0.75	0.73	0.71	0.75	0.73	0.61	0.74
average_precision_score_macro	0.57	0.54	0.57	0.56	0.55	0.50	0.55	0.55	0.55	0.56	..	0.54	0.58	0.56	0.56	0.55	0.54	0.55	0.55	0.40	0.58
average_precision_score_micro	0.57	0.54	0.57	0.56	0.55	0.50	0.55	0.55	0.55	0.56	...	0.54	0.58	0.56	0.56	0.55	0.54	0.55	0.55	0.40	0.58
average_precision_score_weighted	0.57	0.54	0.57	0.56	0.55	0.50	0.55	0.55	0.55	0.56	...	0.54	0.58	0.56	0.56	0.55	0.54	0.55	0.55	0.40	0.58
balanced_accuracy	0.59	0.57	0.63	0.63	0.70	0.57	0.62	0.62	0.58	0.61	.	0.70	0.63	0.64	0.65	0.62	0.70	0.66	0.56	0.70	0.71
f1_score_macro	0.59	0.55	0.64	0.64	0.68	0.56	0.62	0.62	0.58	0.62	..	0.67	0.64	0.65	0.66	0.63	0.67	0.67	0.55	0.60	0.69
f1_score_micro	0.73	0.74	0.75	0.75	0.71	0.73	0.74	0.75	0.74	0.72	..	0.71	0.74	0.75	0.75	0.73	0.71	0.75	0.73	0.61	0.74
f1_score_weighted	0.70	0.68	0.73	0.73	0.73	0.68	0.72	0.72	0.69	0.71	..	0.72	0.73	0.73	0.74	0.72	0.72	0.74	0.67	0.62	0.75
log_loss	0.50	0.52	0.50	0.50	0.55	0.52	0.51	0.51	0.52	0.53	.	0.56	0.50	0.51	0.53	0.51	0.56	0.56	0.51	0.61	0.52
norm_macro_recall	0.18	0.13	0.27	0.26	0.39	0.13	0.23	0.23	0.16	0.22	..	0.39	0.26	0.28	0.29	0.25	0.39	0.33	0.12	0.39	0.41
precision_score_macro	0.65	0.70	0.68	0.68	0.67	0.66	0.68	0.68	0.69	0.64	...	0.67	0.66	0.68	0.68	0.66	0.67	0.69	0.68	0.67	0.69
precision_score_micro	0.73	0.74	0.75	0.75	0.71	0.73	0.74	0.75	0.74	0.72	..	0.71	0.74	0.75	0.75	0.73	0.71	0.75	0.73	0.61	0.74
precision_score_weighted	0.70	0.72	0.73	0.73	0.75	0.70	0.72	0.72	0.72	0.70	..	0.75	0.72	0.73	0.73	0.71	0.75	0.74	0.71	0.78	0.76
recall_score_macro	0.59	0.57	0.63	0.63	0.70	0.57	0.62	0.62	0.58	0.61	..	0.70	0.63	0.64	0.65	0.62	0.70	0.66	0.56	0.70	0.71
recall_score_micro	0.73	0.74	0.75	0.75	0.71	0.73	0.74	0.75	0.74	0.72	.	0.71	0.74	0.75	0.75	0.73	0.71	0.75	0.73	0.61	0.74
recall_score_weighted	0.73	0.74	0.75	0.75	0.71	0.73	0.74	0.75	0.74	0.72	.	0.71	0.74	0.75	0.75	0.73	0.71	0.75	0.73	0.61	0.74
weighted_accuracy	0.82	0.85	0.82	0.83	0.73	0.84	0.83	0.83	0.85	0.90	.	0.71	0.81	0.82	0.81	0.80	0.72	0.81	0.85	0.55	0.76

20 rows × 30 columns

Figure 6-14. Metrics for each iteration in a run

Selecting and testing the best model from the experiment run

To use the best model, you can use the get_output() function (the output is shown in Figure 6-15):

```
best_run, fitted_model = local_run.get_output(metric = "AUC_weighted")

print(best_run)
```

```
In [30]:  best_run, fitted_model = local_run.get_output(metric = "AUC_weighted")
          print(best_run)

          executed in 12.5s, finished 15:53:07 2019-03-25

          Run(Experiment: automl-classification,
          Id: AutoML_37e1a0dc-e7ea-4d87-b7c3-d59e00d5b129_29,
          Type: None,
          Status: Completed)
```

Figure 6-15. Information about the best run

Let's test the model using the test data, and understand the classification metrics from the evaluation, as well as the area under the receiver operating characteristic curve (ROC AUC):

```
from sklearn.metrics import classification_report
from sklearn.metrics import roc_auc_score

y_pred = fitted_model.predict(X_test)

target_names = ['0','1']
print (classification_report(
        y_test,y_pred, target_names=target_names))
print("AUC: " + str(roc_auc_score(y_test,y_pred)))
```

Figure 6-16 shows the output from testing the model using the test data, and the relevant metrics: precision, recall, f1-score, and support for the model.

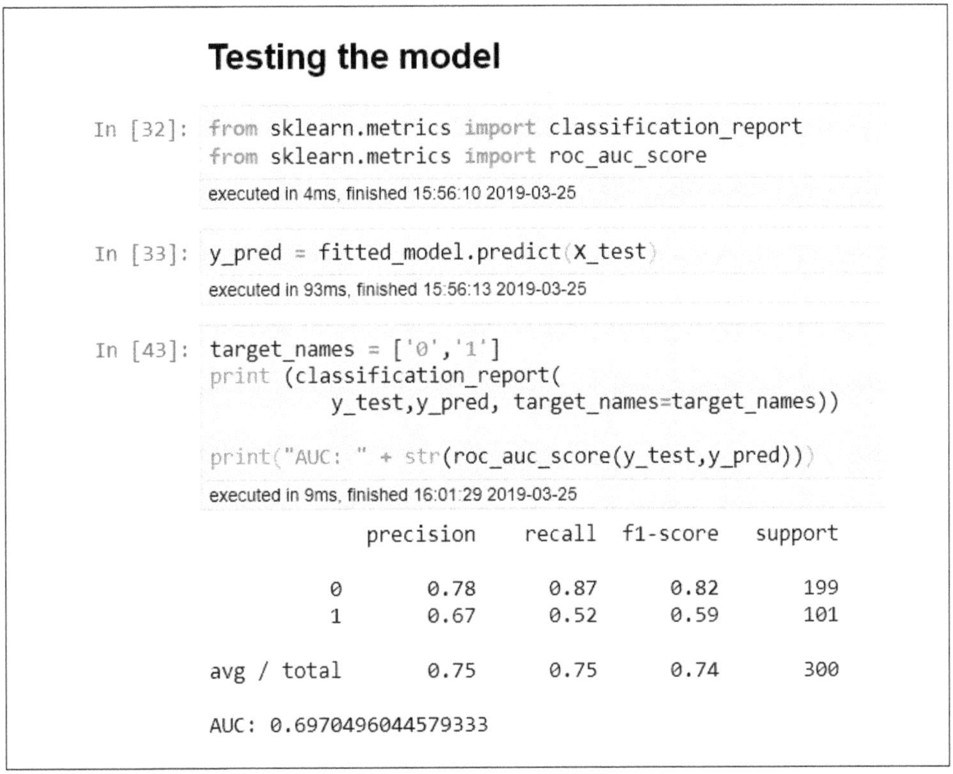

Testing the model

```
In [32]: from sklearn.metrics import classification_report
         from sklearn.metrics import roc_auc_score
```
executed in 4ms, finished 15:56:10 2019-03-25

```
In [33]: y_pred = fitted_model.predict(X_test)
```
executed in 93ms, finished 15:56:13 2019-03-25

```
In [43]: target_names = ['0','1']
         print (classification_report(
                 y_test,y_pred, target_names=target_names))

         print("AUC: " + str(roc_auc_score(y_test,y_pred)))
```
executed in 9ms, finished 16:01:29 2019-03-25

	precision	recall	f1-score	support
0	0.78	0.87	0.82	199
1	0.67	0.52	0.59	101
avg / total	0.75	0.75	0.74	300

AUC: 0.6970496044579333

Figure 6-16. Classification metrics and AUC for the best model selected

Conclusion

In this chapter, you learned how to use automated ML with Azure Machine Learning to find the best classification models for predicting a person's credit risk. You can also use the same approach for identifying the best regression models. After you've identified the best classification/regression models for a task, refer to Chapter 5 to see how to deploy the machine learning models to various environments.

## PART III

How Enterprises Are Using Automated Machine Learning

In this part, you will learn how automated ML is democratizing AI and empowering people across the enterprise to do machine learning with familiar tools.

## CHAPTER 7

Model Interpretability and Transparency with Automated ML

We discussed earlier how building good machine learning models is a pretty time-consuming process. What is a "good" machine learning model? We saw that this is usually defined by performance of the model, as measured by accuracy or similar metrics. As companies get ready to adopt machine learning for business-critical scenarios, interpretability and transparency of machine learning models becomes vital.

In this chapter, we cover key aspects around interpretability and transparency of machine learning that leads to customer trust. Interpretability and transparency become even more important when you are trying to use or customize a machine learning pipeline developed by others, including those generated by Automated Machine Learning systems. Let's take a deeper look at how automated ML on Microsoft Azure Machine Learning enables model interpretability and transparency.

Model Interpretability

Most machine learning models are considered black boxes because it's usually difficult to understand or explain how they work. Without this understanding, it is difficult to trust the model, and therefore difficult to convince executive stakeholders and customers of the business value of machine learning and machine learning–based systems.

Some models, like linear regression, are considered to be fairly straightforward and therefore easy to understand, but as we add more features or use more complicated machine learning models like neural networks, understanding them becomes more and more difficult. Usually, more complex (and not-so-easy-to-understand) models perform much better—that is, they achieve greater accuracy—than those that are simpler, and easier to understand. Figure 7-1 shows this relationship.

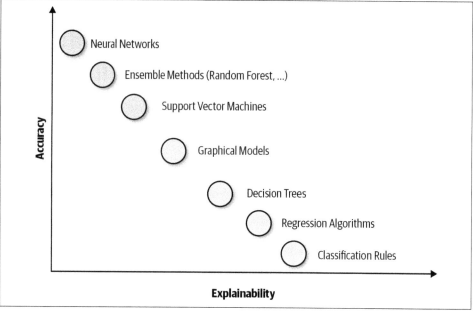

Figure 7-1. Interpretability/explainability versus model performance

Businesses run on transparency and trust, and being able to open the machine learning black box to explain a model helps build transparency and trust. In heavily regulated industries like health care and banking, interpretability and transparency are critical. Here are few real-world scenarios to illustrate the value of interpretability and transparency in machine learning:

- A manufacturing company using machine learning to predict future instrument failure so that it can proactively perform maintenance activity.
  - When you know an instrument is about to fail, what's the most likely cause going to be so that you can quickly perform preventive maintenance?
- A financial institution using machine learning to process loan or credit card applications.
  - How do you know whether the model is doing the right thing?
  - If a customer asks for more details on why their application was rejected, how will you respond to them?
- An online retailer or an independent software vendor (ISV) using machine learning to predict customer churn—in other words, whether a customer is going to stop using their product/service soon.

— What are the key contributors to customer churn?

— How can you prevent customers from churning?

Feature importance is a popular approach used for model interpretability. Feature importance indicates how each input column (or feature) affects the model's predictions. This allows data scientists to explain the resulting model and predictions so that stakeholders can see which data points are most important in the model.

Model Interpretability with Azure Machine Learning

The Azure Machine Learning Python SDK offers various interpretability packages to help you understand feature importance. Using these packages, you can explain machine learning models globally on all data, or locally on a specific data point.

Explainers

There are two sets of explainers in the Azure Machine Learning SDK, specifically the `azureml.explain.model` package: direct explainers and meta explainers.

Direct explainers come from integrated libraries. A popular approach for explaining the output of machine learning model is SHAP (short for "SHapley Additive exPlanations"). The following is a list of the direct explainers available in the SDK:

SHAP Tree Explainer
SHAP's Tree Explainer focuses on trees and ensembles of trees.

SHAP Deep Explainer
Based on the explanation from SHAP, Deep Explainer focuses on deep learning models. TensorFlow models and Keras models using the TensorFlow backend are supported (there is also preliminary support for PyTorch).

SHAP Kernel Explainer
SHAP's Kernel Explainer uses a specially weighted local linear regression to estimate SHAP values for any model.

Mimic Explainer
Mimic Explainer is based on the idea of global surrogate models. A global surrogate model is an intrinsically interpretable model that is trained to approximate the predictions of a black-box model as accurately as possible. You can interpret a surrogate model to draw conclusions about the black-box model.

PFI Explainer
Permutation Feature Importance (PFI) Explainer is a technique used to explain classification and regression models. At a high level, the way it works is by randomly shuffling data one feature at a time for the entire dataset and calculating

how much the performance metric of interest decreases. The larger the change, the more important that feature is.

LIME Explainer
Local interpretable model-agnostic explanations (LIME) Explainer uses the state-of-the-art LIME algorithm to create local surrogate models. Unlike the global surrogate models, LIME focuses on training local surrogate models to explain individual predictions. This is currently available in only the contrib/preview package `azureml.contrib.explain.model`.

HAN Text Explainer
HAN Text Explainer uses a hierarchical attention network for getting model explanations from text data for a given black-box text model. This is currently available only in the contrib/preview package: `azureml.contrib.explain.model`.

Meta explainers automatically select a suitable direct explainer and generate the best explanation information based on the given model and datasets. Currently, the following meta explainers are available in the Azure Machine Learning SDK:

Tabular Explainer
Used with tabular datasets

Text Explainer
Used with text datasets

Image Explainer
Used with image datasets

Text Explainer and Image Explainer are currently available only in the contrib/preview package `azureml.contrib.explain.model`.

In addition to automatically selecting direct explainers, meta explainers develop additional features on top of the underlying libraries and improve the speed and scalability over the direct explainers. Currently `TabularExplainer` employs the following logic to invoke the direct explainers:

1. If it's a tree-based model, apply `TreeExplainer`, else
2. If it's a DNN model, apply `DeepExplainer`, else
3. Treat it as a black-box model and apply `KernelExplainer`.

The intelligence built into `TabularExplainer` will become more sophisticated as more libraries are integrated into the SDK.

Figure 7-2 shows the relationship between direct and meta explainers and which ones are suitable for different types of data. The SDK wraps all of the explainers so that they expose a common API and output format.

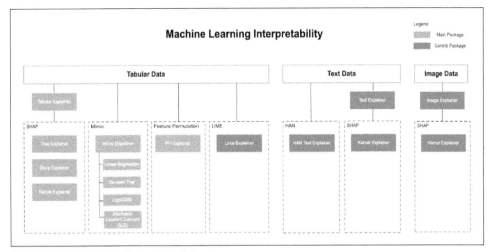

Figure 7-2. Direct and meta explainers

You'll now see how to use these explainers in generating feature importance for the following two scenarios: a regression model trained using sklearn and a classification model trained using automated ML.

Regression model trained using sklearn

We will build a regression model to predict housing prices using the Boston house price dataset from sklearn (*https://oreil.ly/xUiJb*). The dataset has 506 rows, 13 input columns (features), and 1 target column. Here are the input columns:

- CRIM: Per capita crime rate by town
- ZN: Proportion of residential land zoned for lots over 25,000 sq. ft.
- INDUS: Proportion of nonretail business acres per town
- CHAS: Charles River dummy variable (1 if tract bounds river; 0 otherwise)
- NOX: Nitric oxides concentration (parts per 10 million)
- RM: Average number of rooms per dwelling
- AGE: Proportion of owner-occupied units built prior to 1940
- DIS: Weighted distances to five Boston employment centers
- RAD: Index of accessibility to radial highways
- TAX: Full-value property-tax rate per $10,000
- PTRATIO: Student-teacher ratio by town
- B: $1,000 * (Bk-0.63)^2$, where Bk is the proportion of African Americans by town (this dataset is from 1978)

- LSTAT: % lower status of the population

And this is the one target column:

- MEDV: Median value of owner-occupied homes in $1,000s

After loading the dataset and splitting it into train and test sets, we train a simple regression model using sklearn `GradientBoostingRegressor`. Next we'll use `Tabular Explainer` from the `azureml.explain.model` package to generate *global feature importance* for the trained model. After the global explanations are generated, we use the methods `get_ranked_global_values()` and `get_ranked_global_names()` to get ranked feature importance values and the corresponding feature names:

```
from sklearn.ensemble import GradientBoostingRegressor

reg = GradientBoostingRegressor(n_estimators=100, max_depth=4,
                                learning_rate=0.1, loss='huber',
                                random_state=1)

model = reg.fit(x_train, y_train)

from azureml.explain.model.tabular_explainer import TabularExplainer

tabular_explainer = TabularExplainer(model, x_train, features =
                                     boston_data.feature_names)

global_explanation = tabular_explainer.explain_global(x_train)

# Sorted SHAP values
print('Ranked global importance values:
      {}'.format(global_explanation.get_ranked_global_values()))

# Corresponding feature names
print('Ranked global importance names:
      {}'.format(global_explanation.get_ranked_global_names()))

# Display in an easy to understand format
dict(zip(global_explanation.get_ranked_global_names(),
         global_explanation.get_ranked_global_values()))
```

Figure 7-3 shows ranked global feature importance output. This indicates that the LSTAT (% lower status of the population) feature is most influential on the output of the model.

```
Ranked global importance values: [3.2845940819520645, 1.9552656592838449, 1.0785478784887184, 0.6376367601698039, 0.6103384
220260784, 0.5876959735465017, 0.5264915603029366, 0.4625094534084926, 0.22868942459726516, 0.22385390138304972, 0.08371780
876320355, 0.01104462557243398, 0.008271501262553011]
Ranked global importance names: ['LSTAT', 'RM', 'PTRATIO', 'NOX', 'DIS', 'TAX', 'AGE', 'CRIM', 'INDUS', 'B', 'RAD', 'ZN',
'CHAS']

{'LSTAT': 3.2845940819520645,
 'RM': 1.9552656592838449,
 'PTRATIO': 1.0785478784887184,
 'NOX': 0.6376367601698039,
 'DIS': 0.6103384220260784,
 'TAX': 0.5876959735465017,
 'AGE': 0.5264915603029366,
 'CRIM': 0.4625094534084926,
 'INDUS': 0.22868942459726516,
 'B': 0.22385390138304972,
 'RAD': 0.08371780876320355,
 'ZN': 0.01104462557243398,
 'CHAS': 0.008271501262553011}
```

Figure 7-3. Global feature importance

Next, we look at how to compute *local feature importance* for a specific row of data. This is especially relevant at prediction time. We pass one row from the test set to explain_local() method and print the local feature importance:

```
local_explanation = tabular_explainer.explain_local(x_test[0,:])

# Sorted local feature importance information; reflects original feature order
print('sorted local importance names:
        {}'.format(local_explanation.get_ranked_local_names()))

print('sorted local importance values:
        {}'.format(local_explanation.get_ranked_local_values()))

# Display in an easy to understand format
dict(zip(local_explanation.get_ranked_local_names(),
        local_explanation.get_ranked_local_values()))
```

As seen in Figure 7-4, although LSTAT remains as the topmost feature in terms of importance for this specific test record, AGE is the second most impactful feature.

```
sorted local importance names: ['LSTAT', 'AGE', 'PTRATIO', 'NOX', 'B', 'CRIM', 'INDUS', 'ZN', 'CHAS', 'RAD', 'RM', 'DIS',
'TAX']
sorted local importance values: [2.5698109192250715, 1.0130258497483609, 0.6966226461107805, 0.4762715428003659, 0.31406814
097544067, 0.2705529596496711, 0.23477176103309483, 0.01374023248180678, 0.0, -0.09860772253453287, -0.20582340746530353, -
0.43576020523074865, -0.8448627049383619]

{'LSTAT': 2.5698109192250715,
 'AGE': 1.0130258497483609,
 'PTRATIO': 0.6966226461107805,
 'NOX': 0.4762715428003659,
 'B': 0.31406814097544067,
 'CRIM': 0.2705529596496711,
 'INDUS': 0.23477176103309483,
 'ZN': 0.01374023248180678,
 'CHAS': 0.0,
 'RAD': -0.09860772253453287,
 'RM': -0.20582340746530353,
 'DIS': -0.43576020523074865,
 'TAX': -0.8448627049383619}
```

Figure 7-4. Local feature importance

As discussed in Chapter 4, raw data usually goes through multiple transformations before going through the training process. Features produced through this process are called *engineered features*, whereas the raw input columns are known as *raw features*. By default, explainers explain the model in terms of features used for training (i.e., engineered features) and not on the raw features.

However, in most real-world situations, you would like to understand *raw feature importance*. Raw feature importance informs you how each raw input column influences the model prediction, whereas *engineered feature importance* is not directly based on your inputs columns, but on columns generated through transformations on input columns. Hence, raw feature importance is a lot more understandable and actionable than engineered feature importance.

Using the SDK, you can pass your feature transformation pipeline to the explainer to receive raw feature importance. If you skip this, the explainer provides engineered feature importance. In general, any of the transformations on a single column will be supported:

```
from sklearn.pipeline import Pipeline
from sklearn.impute import SimpleImputer
from sklearn.preprocessing import StandardScaler, OneHotEncoder
from sklearn.linear_model import LogisticRegression
from sklearn_pandas import DataFrameMapper

# Assume that we have created two arrays, numerical and categorical,
that hold the numerical and categorical feature names.

numeric_transformations = [([f], Pipeline(steps=[('imputer',
    SimpleImputer(strategy='median')), ('scaler',
    StandardScaler())])) for f in numerical]

categorical_transformations = [([f], OneHotEncoder(handle_unknown='ignore',
    sparse=False)) for f in categorical]

transformations = numeric_transformations + categorical_transformations

# Append model to preprocessing pipeline.
# Now we have a full prediction pipeline.
clf = Pipeline(steps=[('preprocessor', DataFrameMapper(transformations)),
                    ('classifier', LogisticRegression(solver='lbfgs'))])

# clf.steps[-1][1] returns the trained classification model
# Pass transformation as an input to create the explanation object
# "features" and "classes" fields are optional
tabular_explainer = TabularExplainer(clf.steps[-1][1],
    initialization_examples=x_train, features=dataset_feature_names,
    classes=dataset_classes, transformations=transformations)
```

So far, you have seen how to generate feature importance during model training time. It is also important to understand feature importance at inference time for a specific row of data. Let's consider this scenario: suppose that you own a machine learning–powered application to do credit card application processing. If your application rejects a credit card application, you need to explain why the model rejects that specific applicant.

To enable *inference-time feature importance*, the explainer can be deployed along with the original model and can be used at scoring time to provide the local explanation information. Next, we examine how to enable feature importance with the automated ML tool in Azure Machine Learning.

Classification model trained using automated ML

We will use the sklearn iris dataset (*https://oreil.ly/1aaIj*). This is a well-known classification scenario for flowers. There are three classes of flowers and four input features: petal length, petal width, sepal length, and sepal width. The dataset has 150 rows (50 rows per flower class).

After loading the dataset and splitting it into train and test sets, we train a classification model using automated ML. To enable feature importance for each of the models trained by automated ML, we set `model_explainability=True` in AutoMLConfig:

```
automl_config = AutoMLConfig(task = 'classification',
                             debug_log = 'automl_errors.log',
                             primary_metric = 'AUC_weighted',
                             iteration_timeout_minutes = 200,
                             iterations = 10,
                             verbosity = logging.INFO,
                             X = X_train,
                             y = y_train,
                             X_valid = X_test,
                             y_valid = y_test,
                             model_explainability=True,
                             path=project_folder)

local_run = experiment.submit(automl_config, show_output=True)

best_run, fitted_model = local_run.get_output()
```

Because this is a classification problem, you can get not only overall model-level feature importance, but also feature importance per class.

Let's review how to use the `azureml.train.automl.automlexplainer` package to extract feature importance values from models generated in automated ML. We use the best run here as an example, but you can retrieve any run from automated ML training:

```
from azureml.train.automl.automlexplainer import retrieve_model_explanation

shap_values, expected_values, overall_summary, overall_imp,
```

```
                    per_class_summary, per_class_imp = \
                    retrieve_model_explanation(best_run)

# Global model level feature importance
print('Sorted global importance names: {}'.format(overall_imp))
print('Sorted global importance values: {}'.format(overall_summary))

# Global class level feature importance
print('Sorted global class-level importance names: {}'.format(per_class_imp))
print('Sorted global class-level importance values:
      {}'.format(per_class_summary))
```

Figure 7-5 shows the output: global feature importance for the model and class-level feature importance.

```
Sorted global importance names: ['petal length (cm)', 'petal width (cm)', 'sepal width (cm)', 'sepal length (cm)']
Sorted global importance values: [1.831587410708562, 1.7037592703482562, 0.2949730345894476, 0.18709776945585313]
Sorted global class-level importance names: [['petal length (cm)', 'petal width (cm)', 'sepal width (cm)', 'sepal length (c
m)'], ['petal width (cm)', 'petal length (cm)', 'sepal width (cm)', 'sepal length (cm)'], ['petal length (cm)', 'petal lengt
h (cm)', 'sepal length (cm)', 'sepal width (cm)']]
Sorted global class-level importance values: [[2.5871429057233315, 1.4774879358476867, 0.23484031092269503, 0.0037401151029
756766], [1.519816118237217, 1.3746149641274394, 0.5235026623786724, 0.37684034065172145], [2.1139737569598647, 1.533004362
274915, 0.18071285261286232, 0.1265761304669755]]
```

Figure 7-5. Feature importance for automated ML model

In addition to using the SDK to get feature importance values, you can also get it through widget UX in the notebook or Azure portal. Let's see how to do that from widget UX. After automated ML training is complete, you can use RunDetails from the azureml.widgets package to visualize the automated ML training including all of the machine learning pipelines tried, which you can see in Figure 7-6.

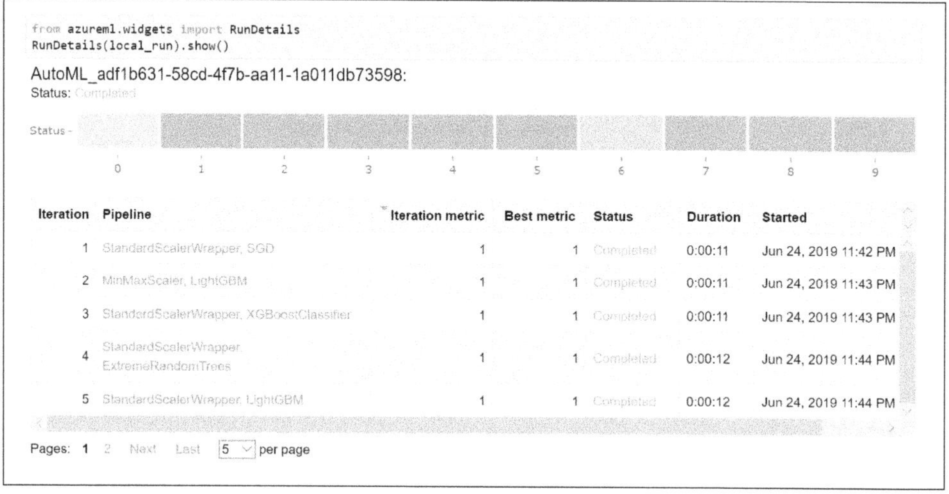

Figure 7-6. Automated ML widget UX

You can click any of the machine learning pipelines to explore more. In addition to a bunch of charts, you will see a feature importance chart. Use the legend to see overall model-level as well as class-level feature importance. In Figure 7-7, you can see that "petal width (cm)" is the most important feature from the overall model perspective, but "sepal width (cm)" is the most important feature for class 1.

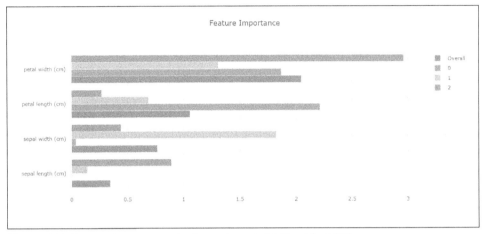

Figure 7-7. Feature importance in the automated ML widget UX

Model Transparency

In the previous section, you learned how feature importance is a powerful way to understand machine learning models. It is also important to understand the training process, from input data leading to the machine learning model. In this section, we will discuss how automated ML makes the end-to-end training process transparent.

Understanding the Automated ML Model Pipelines

As discussed in earlier chapters, automated ML recommends model pipelines with the goal of producing high-quality ML models based on user inputs. Each model pipeline includes the following steps:

1. Data preprocessing and feature engineering
2. Model training based on selected algorithm and hyperparameter values

With automated ML, you can analyze steps of each recommended pipeline before using them in your application or scenario. This transparency not only allows you to trust the model better, but also enables you to customize it further. For details on how to get visibility into the end-to-end process, refer to Chapter 4, which covers all of the steps in automated ML–recommended machine learning pipelines.

Guardrails

In previous chapters, you saw that automated ML makes it easy to get started with machine learning by automating most of the iterative and time-consuming steps. In addition, there are many best practices that you need to apply to achieve reliable results. *Guardrails* help users understand potential issues with their data and training model, so they know what to expect and can correct the issues for improved results.

Following are some common issues to be aware of:

Missing values

As we've discussed in earlier chapters, real-world data isn't clean and could be missing a lot of values. Before using it for machine learning, data with missing values needs to be "fixed." Various techniques can be used to fix missing values, from dropping entire rows to using various techniques to intelligently populate missing values based on the rest of the data; this is called *imputation*.

Class imbalance

Class imbalance is a major problem in machine learning because most machine learning algorithms assume that data is equally distributed. In the case of imbalanced data, majority classes dominate over minority classes, causing the machine learning models to be more biased toward majority classes. This results in poor classification of minority classes. Some real-world examples involve anomaly detection, fraud detection, and disease detection.

Sampling is a commonly used strategy to overcome class imbalance. There are two ways to sample:

Undersampling

Balancing the dataset by removing some instance of majority class.

Oversampling

Adding similar instances of the minority class to balance.

Data leakage

Data leakage is another key problem when building machine learning models. This occurs when the training dataset includes information that would not be available at the time of prediction. Because the actual outcome is already known (due to leakage), the model performance will be almost perfect for the training data but will be very bad during prediction. There are a few tricks you can use to overcome data leakage:

Remove leaky features

Use simple rule-based models to identify leaky features and remove them.

Hold out dataset
> Hold back an unseen test set as a final sanity check of your model before you use it.

Add noise
> Add noise to input data to smooth out the effects of possibly leaky features.

As you can see, understanding and safeguarding against common issues like these can be critical to the performance of the model as well as transparency to users. Automated ML offers guardrails to show and protect against common issues and will continue to add more sophisticated ones over time.

Conclusion

In this chapter, we discussed two key aspects that become very important when establishing trust in a trained machine learning model: interpretability and transparency. Almost every company or team using machine learning models requires the models to be interpretable and transparent–to a degree–to gain confidence.

You learned how to take advantage of interpretability/explainability features by using the Azure Machine Learning Python SDK, as well as the automated ML Python SDK and widget UX. We also touched upon gaining visibility into end-to-end model-training pipelines as well as pitfalls to avoid, and why setting up guardrails against these pitfalls is important to ensure the transparency of your model.

## CHAPTER 8

Automated ML for Developers

Earlier, you learned how to use the automated ML tool in Azure Machine Learning with Jupyter Notebooks. In this chapter, you'll learn how to use automated ML in other environments: Azure Databricks, ML.NET, and SQL Server.

Azure Databricks and Apache Spark

Azure Databricks is a fast, easy, and collaborative Apache Spark–based analytics platform. It is a managed Spark service in Azure and integrates with various Azure services. This means that Azure manages not only the Spark cluster nodes, but also the Spark application running on top of it. It has other helpful features, as follows:

- Azure Databricks, with its goal of improving productivity for users, is designed to be scalable, secure, and easy to manage. It has a collaborative workspace, shared among users who have appropriate permissions. Users can share multiple notebooks, clusters, and libraries from within the workspace.

- The Azure Databricks workspace is a single place where data engineers, data scientists, and business analysts can work with all of the required libraries. The data sources can be available in the same workspace as well.

- In an Azure Databricks workspace, authentication and authorization is based on a user's Azure Active Directory (Azure AD) login. Important from a governance perspective is that it's easy to add or remove a user from the Azure Databricks workspace, and users can be given different permissions, as a reader, contributor, or owner. And it's important from a security perspective that an Azure Databricks cluster deploys in Azure Virtual Network by default and it can be changed to a customer's VNet.

Apache Spark (https://spark.apache.org/) is currently the most popular open source analytics engine for big data processing. You can use Scala, Python, R, or SQL to write Spark-based applications. It's also fast: with Spark, you can improve performance 10 to 100 times over traditional big data technologies because it does some computation in memory instead of reading data from disk. As shown in Figure 8-1, Spark offers powerful libraries like `MLlib` for distributed machine learning, and Spark SQL for distributed SQL and other libraries on top of the core Spark application.

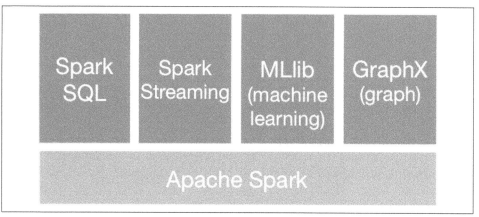

Figure 8-1. Apache Spark stack (source: https://spark.apache.org/)

We'll begin by creating a workspace via the Azure portal (Figure 8-2).

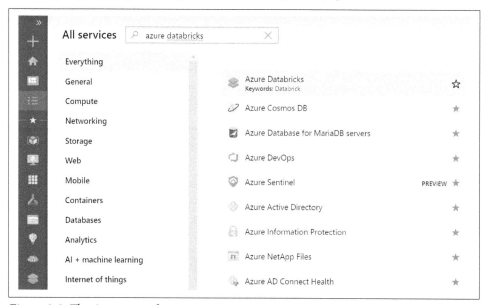

Figure 8-2. The Azure portal

You can search for Azure Databricks or use the Analytics menu option (Figure 8-3).

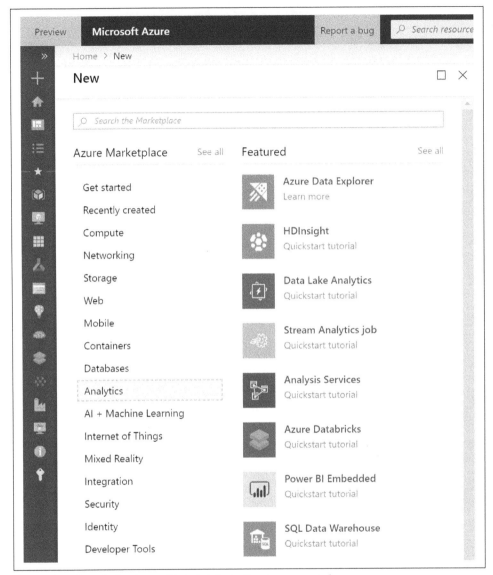

Figure 8-3. Search for Azure Databricks in the Azure portal

Figure 8-4 shows the options for creating the workspace.

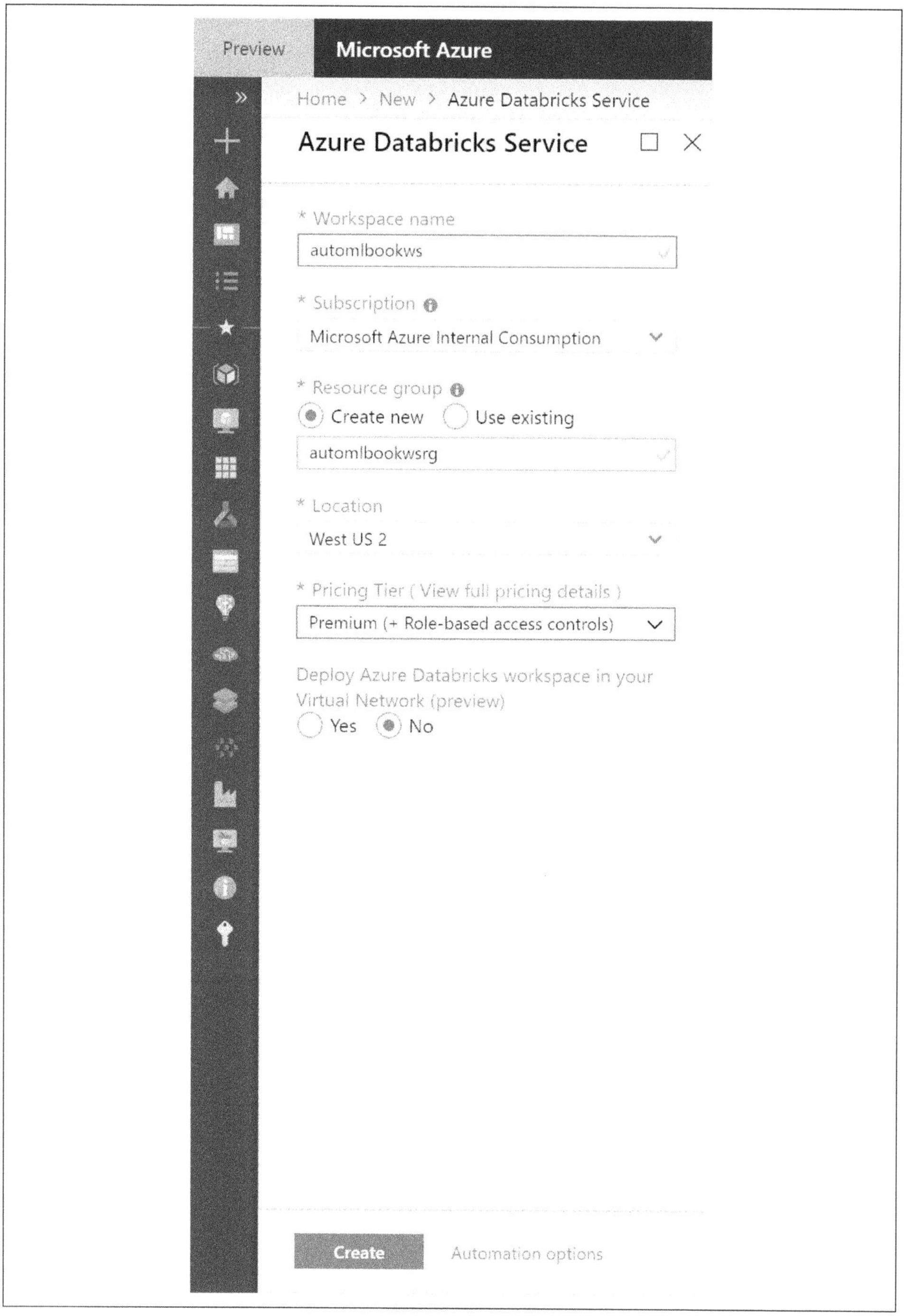

Home > New > Azure Databricks Service

Azure Databricks Service   □ ✕

* Workspace name

```
automlbookws                          ✓
```

* Subscription ❶

```
Microsoft Azure Internal Consumption    ∨
```

* Resource group ❶
(•) Create new   ( ) Use existing

```
automlbookwsrg                        ✓
```

* Location

```
West US 2                             ∨
```

* Pricing Tier (View full pricing details)

```
Premium (+ Role-based access controls)  ∨
```

Deploy Azure Databricks workspace in your
Virtual Network (preview)
( ) Yes (•) No

Create   Automation options

Figure 8-4. Provide details in the Azure Databricks pane

The workspace setup process only takes about a minute:

1. Name the workspace and select the appropriate Azure subscription.

2. Create a new resource group, or an existing resource group.

3. Select a region that will host this workspace. It should have enough quota assigned for your subscription.

4. Select the pricing tier. For this exercise, select Premium.

5. Keep Custom VNET set to No.

Once this is done, the overview page opens, as shown in Figure 8-5.

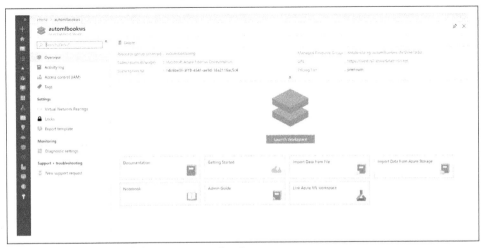

Figure 8-5. Overview of the Azure Databricks resource

From the overview page, click Launch Workspace to open the Azure Databricks workspace page, shown in Figure 8-6. This workspace will have our cluster, notebooks, and related assets. This workspace can be the central place for people who want to run notebooks to do advanced analytics with your data. As we mentioned earlier, you can sign in using your Azure AD credentials. On the left side of the workspace are the options to get data, create clusters, and more.

Figure 8-6. The Azure Databricks workspace

Let's begin by creating a cluster, as shown in Figure 8-7. A Databricks cluster has *driver* and *worker* nodes. When creating a cluster, you provide a cluster name, a Databricks runtime, worker type, and driver type. You can select these values based on the type of experiment that you plan to run. For example, for a large dataset, the VM type should have more memory.

Figure 8-7. The cluster creation page

The cluster uses underlying Azure virtual machines (VMs). As Figure 8-8 shows, you can pick and choose the VM type based on the memory and CPU for the worker and driver type.

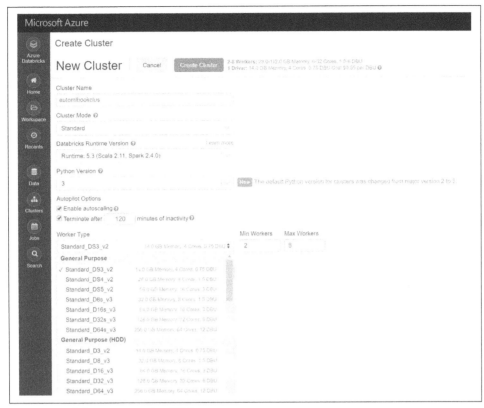

Figure 8-8. Selecting a worker VM type

You now need to consider two autopilot options: autoscaling and autoterminate (Figure 8-9). Setting a time limit for when the cluster will terminate helps you to avoid paying for the cluster when it is not in use. Enabling autoscaling allows you to increase or decrease the compute capacity on demand based on the resources needed.

It can take 10 to 15 minutes to configure your cluster for the first time. This includes installing the libraries that you want to set up for the cluster. For automated ML, install `azureml-sdk[automl]` on Databricks runtime 5.4 and higher.

Figure 8-9. Cluster configuration in the Azure Databricks workspace

For older runtimes, you can install azureml-sdk[autom_databricks], as shown in
Figure 8-10. This is a single package that has everything needed to run automated ML
on Azure Databricks. You can install it from the libraries page.

Figure 8-10. Specifying the automated ML PyPi package

If everything goes well, after the cluster is running and a library is installed on it, your page should like Figure 8-11.

Figure 8-11. Library status

Now let's look at the data options. Select the Data option from the pane on the left, as shown in Figure 8-12.

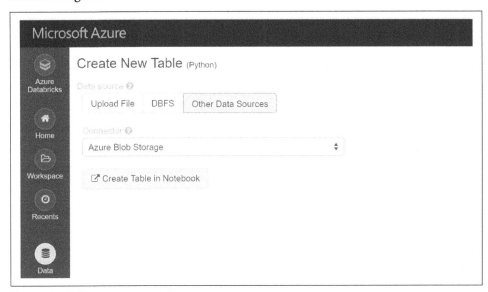

Figure 8-12. Data sources options

You can bring data into your Azure Databricks workspace in multiple ways. Different templates are available to easily start connecting to various data sources. Let's explore the simplest option of connecting to Azure Blob storage, as shown in Figures 8-13 and 8-14 Figure 8-13. We provide the credentials to connect to the storage. The result is a dataframe.

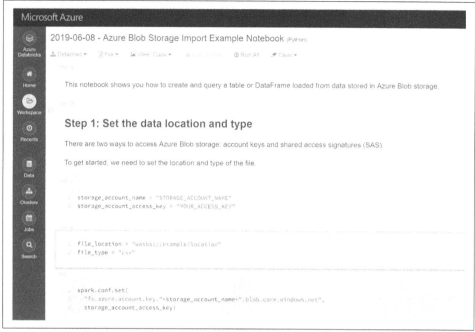

Figure 8-13. A sample notebook for data, part 1

Figure 8-14. A sample notebook for data, part 2

You can use this dataframe for further data preparation. Let's now import a notebook to this Azure Databricks workspace so that you can write machine learning code. You can import a notebook by importing a file or from a URL, as shown in Figure 8-15.

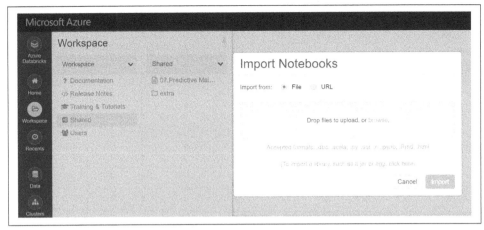

Figure 8-15. Importing a notebook in the workspace

After you import the Notebook, you can attach the cluster to it, as shown in Figure 8-16. Just to read a notebook, you don't need a cluster attached to it, but you need a cluster to execute code.

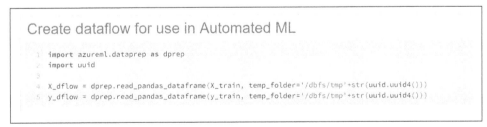

Figure 8-16. Attaching a cluster to the notebook

After you've attached this notebook to your cluster, it can execute the code. To use automated ML, your dataframe must be converted into a dataflow object, as shown in Figure 8-17. This is sample code to convert it.

Create dataflow for use in Automated ML

```
1  import azureml.dataprep as dprep
2  import uuid
3
4  X_dflow = dprep.read_pandas_dataframe(X_train, temp_folder='/dbfs/tmp'+str(uuid.uuid4()))
5  y_dflow = dprep.read_pandas_dataframe(y_train, temp_folder='/dbfs/tmp'+str(uuid.uuid4()))
```

Figure 8-17. Converting a Pandas dataframe to dataflow

After you have a dataflow object, the steps to run automated ML are the same as running a notebook on Jupyter, except for a couple of configuration parameters; Figure 8-18 shows a sample. You can find more details on this Microsoft documentation page (*http://bit.ly/2k9J7qS*).

Configure Automated ML

You can use these params. All params in Azure Doc - https://docs.microsoft.com/en-us/python/api/azureml-train-automl/azureml.train.automl.automlconfig?view=azure-ml-py

Property	Description
task	classification or regression or forecasting
primary_metric	This is the metric that you want to optimize. Classification supports the following primary metrics: accuracy AUC_weighted average_precision_score_weighted norm_macro_recall precision_score_weighted
primary_metric	This is the metric that you want to optimize. Regression supports the following primary metrics: spearman_correlation normalized_root_mean_squared_error r2_score normalized_mean_absolute_error
iteration_timeout_minutes	Time limit in minutes for each iteration.
iterations	Number of iterations. In each iteration AutoML trains a specific pipeline with the data.
max_cores_per_iteration	Default is 1 if not specified else give max cores of your VM. Not every algorithm will use multiple cores.
n_cross_validations	Number of cross validation splits. Do not use this when explicit validation set is provided.
spark_context	Spark Context object. for Databricks, use spark_context=sc
max_concurrent_iterations	Maximum number of iterations to execute in parallel. This should be <= number of worker nodes in your Azure Databricks cluster.
X	(sparse) array-like, shape = [n_samples, n_features]. For Azure Databricks, this has to be a dataflow.
y	(sparse) array-like, shape = [n_samples,]. Multi-class targets. For Azure Databricks, this has to be a dataflow.

Figure 8-18. Sample configuration settings for automated ML

After you submit the experiment for training, you get an outcome that you can view in the Azure portal, as shown in Figure 8-19. Here, we show the summary and the primary metric of each run. You can track the results in a single Azure Machine Learning service workspace independent of which environment that you use to run it.

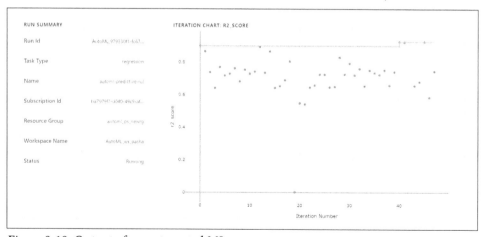

Figure 8-19. Output of an automated ML

After you complete the training, look at the hyperparameters used in the run. Figure 8-20 presents the code for printing the parameters. You can run this code in any environment; it is not specific to Azure Databricks.

Hyper parameters of best model

```
1  #The fitted_model is a python object and you can read the different properties of the object.
2  #The following shows printing hyperparameters for each step in the pipeline.
3
4  from pprint import pprint
5
6  def print_model(model, prefix=""):
7      for step in model.steps:
8          print(prefix + step[0])
9          if hasattr(step[1], 'estimators') and hasattr(step[1], 'weights'):
10             pprint({'estimators': list(e[0] for e in step[1].estimators), 'weights': step[1].weights})
11             print()
12             for estimator in step[1].estimators:
13                 print_model(estimator[1], estimator[0]+ ' - ')
14         else:
15             pprint(step[1].get_params())
16             print()
17
18  print_model(fitted_model)
```

Figure 8-20. Sample code for getting hyperparameters

The output will be like that shown in Figure 8-21 (this is with respect to the model trained in your example notebook). This presents some of the parameters used in training the model.

The notebook to try the full experiment is available on this book's GitHub repository (*https://github.com/PracticalAutomatedMachineLearning/Azure*).

```
MaxAbsScaler
{'copy': True}

LightGBMRegressor
{'boosting_type': 'gbdt',
 'class_weight': None,
 'colsample_bytree': 1,
 'importance_type': 'split',
 'learning_rate': 0.09474210526315789,
 'max_bin': 255,
 'max_depth': 8,
 'min_child_samples': 130,
 'min_child_weight': 0.001,
 'min_split_gain': 0.894736842105263,
 'n_estimators': 800,
 'n_jobs': 1,
 'num_leaves': 31,
 'objective': None,
 'random_state': None,
 'reg_alpha': 0.375,
 'reg_lambda': 0.44999999999999996,
 'silent': True,
 'subsample': 0.75,
 'subsample_for_bin': 200000,
 'subsample_freq': 0,
 'verbose': -1}
```

Figure 8-21. Sample hyperparameters

Now that you've used an Azure Databricks cluster as your compute for training with automated ML, let's see how you can use remote compute from within an Azure Databricks notebook. This is another option that you can use for automated ML training. You might want to use an Azure Databricks cluster for data preparation using Spark and then instead of using the worker nodes from the same cluster, you can use a remote compute option. It can be a viable scenario when your Azure Databricks cluster is being used for other tasks or doesn't have enough worker nodes capacity. This approach can sometimes be more economical, depending on the experiment.

You can find a sample notebook for using remote compute at *http://bit.ly/2lJzVtq*.

ML.NET

Let's learn another way of using automated ML. If you know Visual Studio and are familiar with C#.NET and are interested in building machine learning models but might not know Python, you can use automated ML on ML.NET. To install ML.NET:

1. First install a Terminal on your laptop or use the Terminal in Visual Studio code (installer found on the Visual Studio site (*https://code.visualstudio.com/*); download the appropriate setup). This works on Linux, Windows, or Mac.

2. Next, install .NET Core SDK (*not* Runtime). To install the SDK, download the installer (*https://oreil.ly/mUIJu*).

3. If you need to, restart the Terminal for these changes to take effect.

4. After you finish this setup, run the `dotnet tool install -g mlnet` command in your Terminal.

5. When installation is complete, test whether `mlnet` has been installed successfully by running the `mlnet` command in your Terminal.

6. Next, to start using ML.NET, download the dataset to the laptop on which you installed `mlnet`. In this case, you will use the same NASA dataset we used in previous experiments. You can start the training by giving a simple command on the Terminal as follows:

   ```
   mlnet auto-train --task regression --dataset "df_new.csv"
       --label-column-name rul
   ```

This training takes the default configuration for automated ML. When the training is complete, you will see the results in the same Terminal as that shown in Figure 8-22.

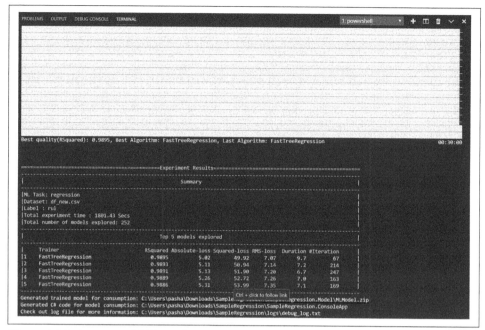

Figure 8-22. Automated ML results

Currently, automated ML on ML.NET with CLI supports the following:

- Binary classification
- Multiclass classification
- Regression

You can also change the default configuration by using the following command on the Terminal:

```
mlnet auto-train
```

It will give a list of the various parameters available to customize. For example, the default training time is 30 minutes, but you can change that based on your needs.

The experiment generates the following assets in the output folder:

- A serialized model ZIP ("best model") for doing our predictions
- C# solution with the following:
  — C# code to predict using the generated model, which can be integrated in your app
  — C# code with the training code used to generate the model as a reference

— A log file with information of all iterations across the multiple algorithms evaluated

You can also call the APIs directly in Visual Studio without using the CLI. It will use the same core automated ML technology as the CLI. Next, let's look at how to use SQL Server to train an automated ML model.

SQL Server

In true democratization style, automated ML is also available to SQL users. We don't need to know Python for that. To get started, we will utilize the ability to run Python code in SQL Server 2017. We can use the *sp_execute_external_script* stored procedure to call AutoML.

You can use SQL Server Management Studio or Azure Data Studio for running automated ML experiments. To give this a try, follow the steps listed in this post on Microsoft's SQL Server Blog (*https://oreil.ly/H7Wyh*).

Conclusion

In this chapter, you learned how to use automated ML from within Azure Databricks, ML.NET, and SQL Server. In Chapter 9, you'll learn how to use Azure UI and Power BI for automated ML.

Automated ML for Everyone

So far, you've seen how data scientists can use the automated ML capability in Microsoft Azure Machine Learning to build machine learning models using the Azure Machine Learning Python SDK. Not everyone has the data science expertise or is familiar with Python. Figure 9-1 shows data from a recent Gartner study indicating lack of skills as the top challenge or barrier in the adoption of artificial intelligence (AI) and machine learning.

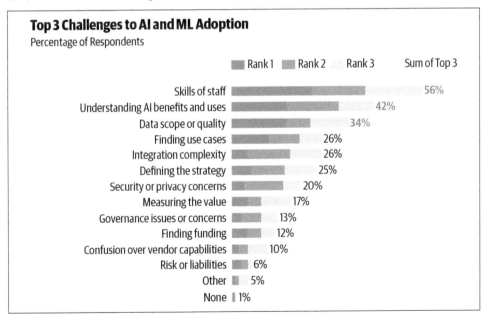

Figure 9-1. Top AI and ML adoption challenges

What if we can remove this barrier? Given the increasing demand for AI and machine learning, people in various departments and roles are becoming interested and involved. Here are a few examples of roles in which people would love to build machine learning models but lack the expertise or familiarity with Python (or other programming languages like R):

- Domain experts or Subject Matter Experts (SMEs)
- Citizen data scientists
- Data analysts
- Data engineers
- Developers

There needs to be a simpler way to use automated ML—ideally, no-code experiences in familiar interfaces instead of having to learn new tools and techniques. In this chapter, we focus on how automated ML is being made available to users who are not experts in machine learning, with the goal of democratizing it.

Azure Portal UI

Although businesses are beginning to fully realize the potential of machine learning, they are also realizing that it requires advanced data science skills that are difficult to find. Many business domain experts have a general understanding of machine learning and predictive analytics; however, they prefer not to delve into the depths of statistics or coding, which are required when working with traditional machine learning tools. This is where we think the Azure portal UI, or Azure UI, will help.

To begin with automated ML in Azure UI, first create an Azure Machine Learning workspace and then create an automated ML experiment. We've covered these steps in earlier chapters, so let's use the same workspace and create a new experiment, as shown in Figure 9-2.

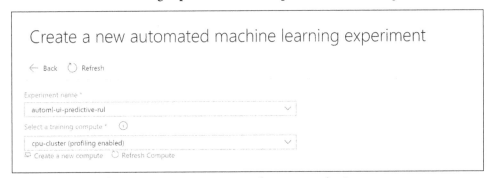

Figure 9-2. Creating a new automated ML experiment

Provide a name for your experiment. You must provide a training compute name. This is an Azure Machine Learning managed compute that will run the experiment. You can also use an existing experiment and compute, as shown in Figure 9-3.

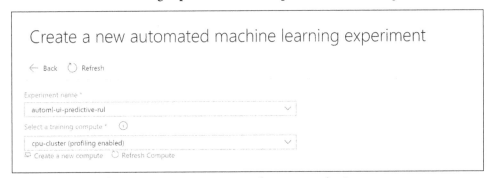

Figure 9-3. Providing an experiment name and compute selection

Next, select the Storage account that has the data for our training. As shown in Figure 9-4, you are asked to pick a comma-separated values (CSV) file from a Blob storage container that will have the full dataset including the prediction label column. This dataset is available at the GitHub repository for this book (*https://github.com/ PracticalAutomatedMachineLearning/Azure*).

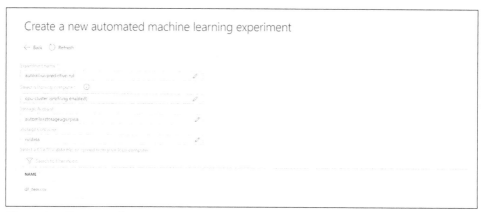

Figure 9-4. Dataset selection

Select the sensor data from NASA's turbofan engine dataset. Once you have selected your dataset, you can preview the data and select columns that you think are relevant for the experiment, as shown in Figure 9-5.

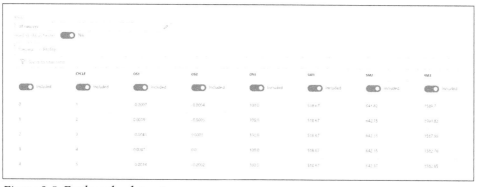

Figure 9-5. Explore the dataset

You can also see the profile of your dataset to understand key characteristics for every column within it, as shown in Figure 9-6. You can see Min, Max, and other types of profiling in the dataset.

Figure 9-6. Dataset profiling

In this experiment, we will not include the index column because it won't add value for the prediction. As shown in Figure 9-7, select Regression as the experiment type.

Figure 9-7. Excluding columns for training

Every automated ML experiment needs a label column. In this case, choose "rul" as the label column, as shown in Figure 9-8. This represents *remaining useful life* of the turbofan engine.

Prediction Task * ⓘ
Regression ⌄

Target column * ⓘ
rul ⌄

Figure 9-8. Select the task and target column

You'll need to change some of the Advanced Settings for this experiment. Use "r2_score" as the metric, which is a common metric for regression-type problems. Next, change the "Training job time" to 30 minutes and "Max number of iterations" to 50. In real life, you might want to set the training job time to 120 minutes and maximum iterations to at least 100 to get good results.

Leave the remaining parameters as is. Figure 9-9 shows these settings.

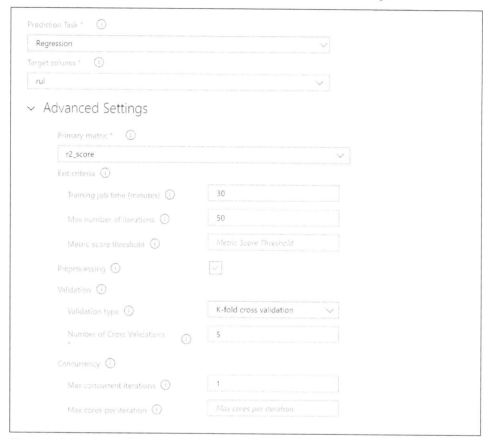

Figure 9-9. Automated ML settings

Click Start to commence the training. Figure 9-10 shows a pop-up with the new run ID.

Figure 9-10. An automated ML run getting started

Initially, when the run starts, it will begin preparing the compute for the experiment, as shown in Figure 9-11. This can take a few minutes.

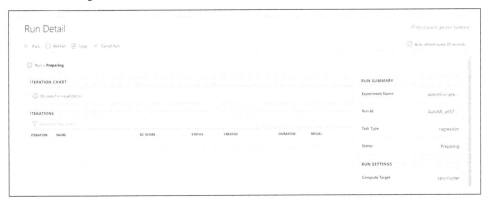

Figure 9-11. Run in preparation

When the training is running, you will see the list of models ranked based on the metric. You can also see how many iterations have been completed. The UI autorefreshes, as shown in Figure 9-12.

Figure 9-12. Training in progress

After a few minutes, you see the experiment has completed and can see a nice chart with all iterations, as shown in Figure 9-13.

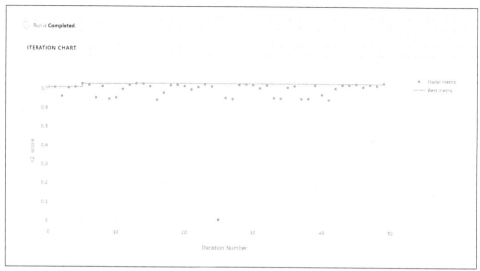

Figure 9-13. View of completed training

You will also see a table with a list of iterations sorted based on highest to lowest *r2_score* metric, as shown in Figure 9-14.

ITERATIONS

ITERATION	NAME	R2 SCORE	STATUS	CREATED	DURATION	MODEL
49	VotingEnsemble	0.7332332525935767	Completed	6/24/2019, 7:54:23 PM	00:01:18	↓ Download
13	MinMaxScaler, GradientBoosting	0.7304360141358007	Completed	6/24/2019, 7:31:59 PM	00:00:36	↓ Download
14	SparseNormalizer, LightGBM	0.7292446283886358	Completed	6/24/2019, 7:32:51 PM	00:00:25	↓ Download
45	RobustScaler, GradientBoosting	0.7288055549308444	Completed	6/24/2019, 7:52:25 PM	00:00:41	↓ Download
5	StandardScalerWrapper, XGBoostRegressor	0.7277117146363592	Completed	6/24/2019, 7:28:01 PM	00:00:29	↓ Download
23	MinMaxScaler, GradientBoosting	0.726889835626664	Completed	6/24/2019, 7:36:30 PM	00:03:32	↓ Download
29	StandardScalerWrapper, ExtremeRandomTr...	0.7263580100731739	Completed	6/24/2019, 7:42:22 PM	00:00:38	↓ Download
47	RobustScaler, ExtremeRandomTrees	0.7259317312024753	Completed	6/24/2019, 7:53:19 PM	00:00:38	↓ Download
44	StandardScalerWrapper, ExtremeRandomTr...	0.7242772179262411	Completed	6/24/2019, 7:51:53 PM	00:00:35	↓ Download
28	StandardScalerWrapper, ExtremeRandomTr...	0.7238579219384109	Completed	6/24/2019, 7:41:30 PM	00:00:36	↓ Download

⏮ ◀ 1 2 3 4 5 ▶ ⏭

Figure 9-14. View of all iterations

You can look at details of each run by clicking its name. You can see graphs and metrics that help you to understand the model better. For example, during iteration 49, as shown in Figures 9-15 and 9-16, you can see the predicted versus true values as well as the metric associated with the model evaluation.

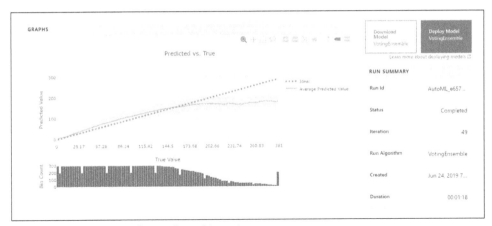

Figure 9-15. Summary for a selected iteration

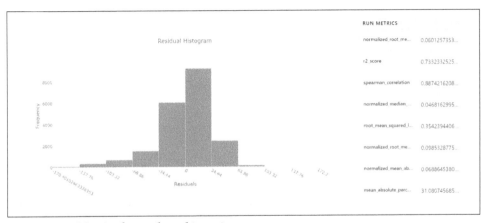

Figure 9-16. Metrics for a selected iteration

As shown in Figure 9-17, you can download the best-trained model associated with the experiment, or from any of these iterations, and deploy it. You can do this in Azure or any suitable environment. After you've downloaded it, this model is in the form of a *.pkl* file. You can also click the Deploy Best Model button instead of manually looking at the table.

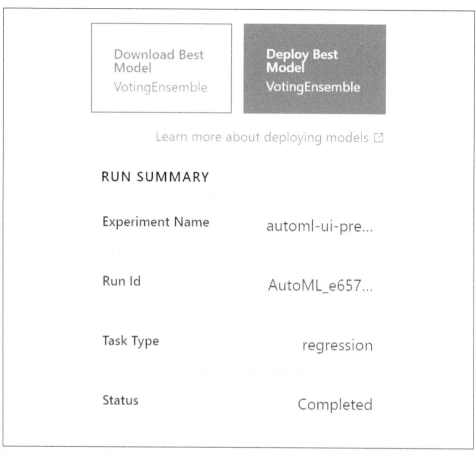

Figure 9-17. Download or deploy the best model

The steps to deploy the model appear when you click the Deploy Best Model button after the experiment has completed running, as shown in Figure 9-18.

The steps for model deployment are the same across the Azure Machine Learning service, independent of the method used to train the machine learning model. Chapter 5 covers deployment, so we don't go in the details of it here.

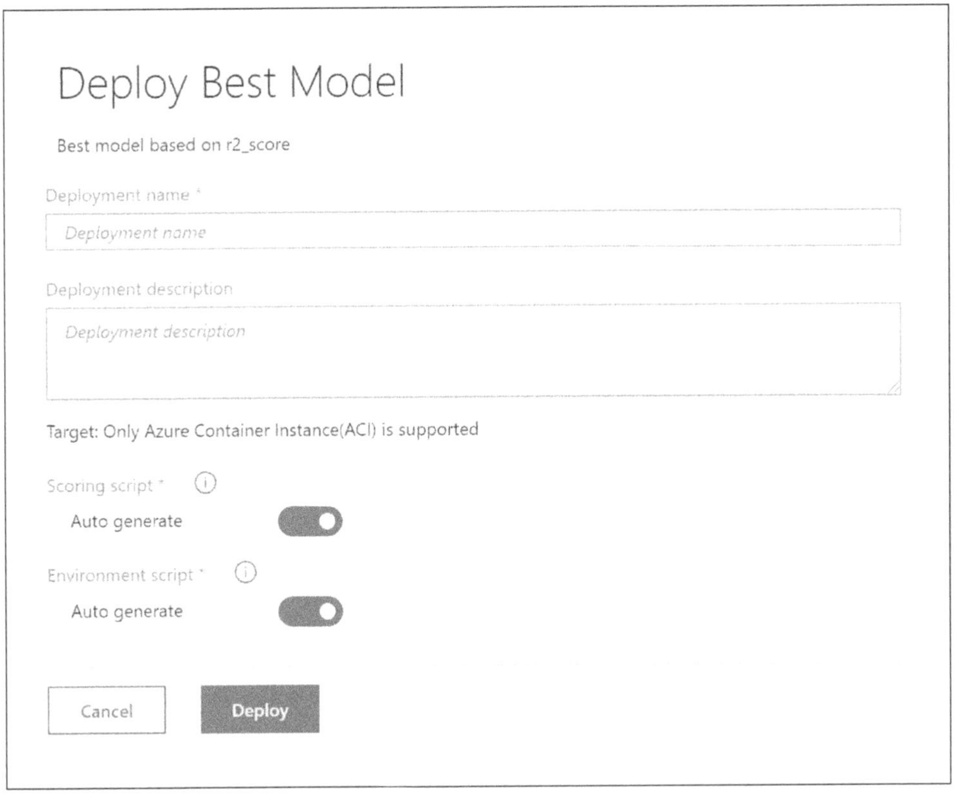

Deploy Best Model

Best model based on r2_score

Deployment name *

> Deployment name

Deployment description

> Deployment description

Target: Only Azure Container Instance(ACI) is supported

Scoring script * ⓘ

    Auto generate   🔘

Environment script * ⓘ

    Auto generate   🔘

  Cancel   **Deploy**

Figure 9-18. Deploying the best model

Next, let's look at how to use Power BI to train an automated ML model.

Power BI

Many data analysts and BI professionals use Power BI for metrics, dashboards, and analysis purposes, but they're looking to take advantage of machine learning to create intelligent experiences and processes.

We'll use the same NASA dataset and learn how to build machine learning models in Power BI using automated ML.

Preparing the Data

As a first step, you need to create a new dataflow in Power BI. Load the NASA dataset using file *Chap_9_PBI_Democratizing_machine_learning_with_AutomatedML.csv* from *http://bit.ly/2meKHs8*.

Go through a new dataflow creation and create a new entity. Power BI dataflows support importing data of many formats and sources, as shown in Figure 9-19. For this experiment, choose the Text/CSV option.

Figure 9-19. Data source selection

Select the dataset path as shown in Figure 9-20.

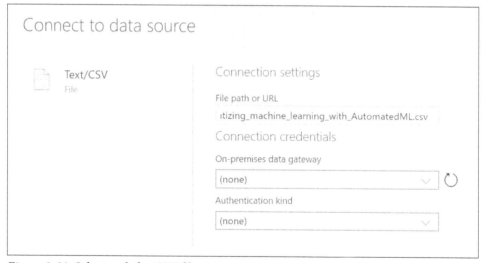

Figure 9-20. Select path for CSV file

Review the data in the newly created entity and then click "Save & close," as demonstrated in Figure 9-21.

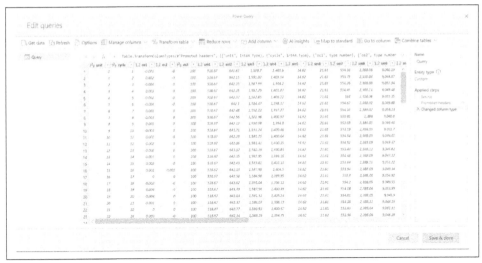

Figure 9-21. Reviewing the data

Automated ML Training

Now, you have a data entity ready to go. You will notice a brain icon in the options for the newly created entity. You can create a new machine learning model by clicking this option, as shown in Figure 9-22.

Figure 9-22. Adding a machine learning model

Next, you'll go through the automated ML authoring steps. Given that the focus is on data analysts and BI professionals who might not have sophisticated data science expertise, this process is very simple. The first step is to choose the data entity (which is autoselected here because we started from that data entity) and the label column that you want to train on. This is shown in Figure 9-23.

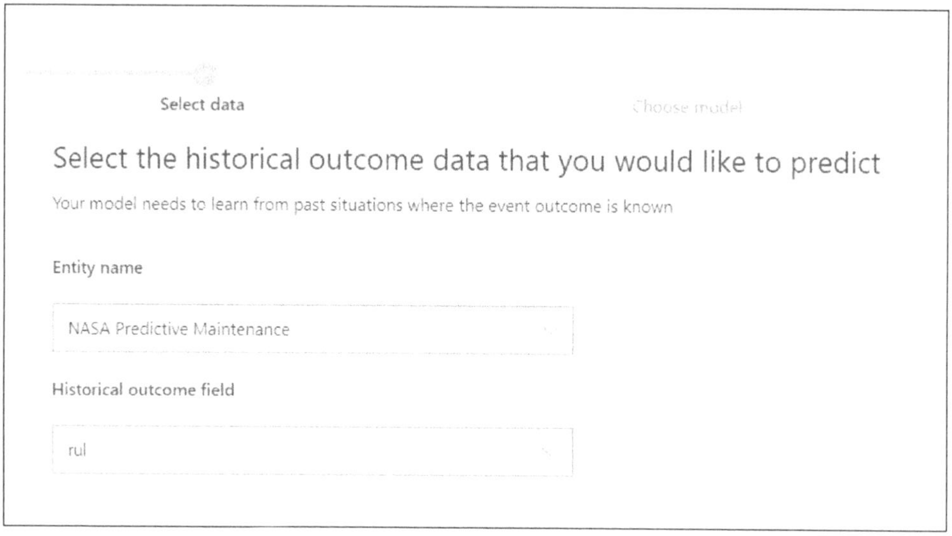

Figure 9-23. *Selecting the data entity and label column*

The system will try to analyze the label column and recommend the appropriate model type. In this case, it is a regression model, as shown in Figure 9-24.

Figure 9-24. *A model type recommendation*

You also have flexibility to choose a different model type if you want, as shown in Figure 9-25.

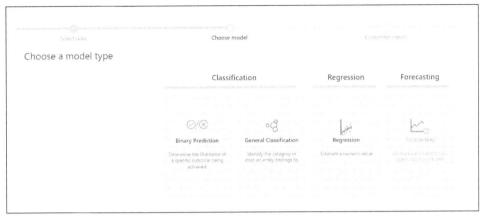

Figure 9-25. Model type selection

Going ahead with modeling this as a regression problem, the next step is to select input features. The system will suggest features, but you have the option to select the ones that you prefer, as shown in Figure 9-26. You can manually deselect a column like "unit," which is not helpful for predictions.

Figure 9-26. Feature selection

In the final step, shown in Figure 9-27, you provide the model with a name and submit it for training.

Figure 9-27. Starting training

This is when automated ML is invoked to train multiple models with the goal of producing a good one for this scenario.

Understanding the Best Model

When the training is complete, you will receive a notification with a link to a report that can help you to more clearly understand the best model as well as the training process.

For the best model, Figure 9-28 shows metrics and details of model performance. Unlike Azure UI that you saw earlier, Power BI directly gives you the best model to simplify decision making.

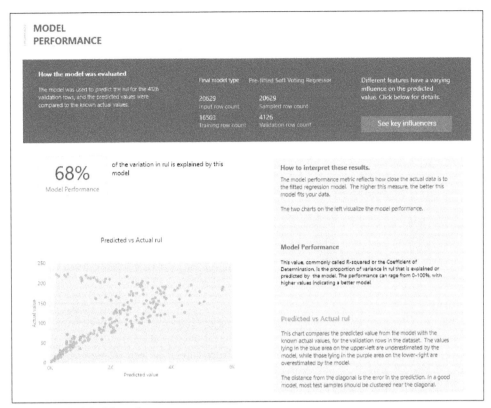

Figure 9-28. Model performance

Figure 9-29 demonstrates how this report also provides details on featurization as well as algorithm and hyperparameter values for the best model.

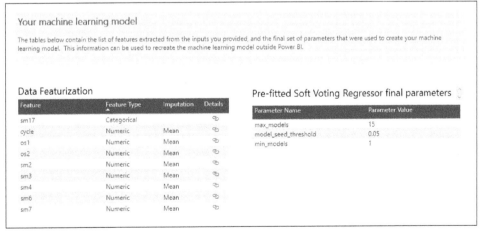

Figure 9-29. Featurization and algorithm/hyperparameters

In this example, the best model is an Ensemble model, and so we get to see more details on the composition of this model, as depicted in Figure 9-30.

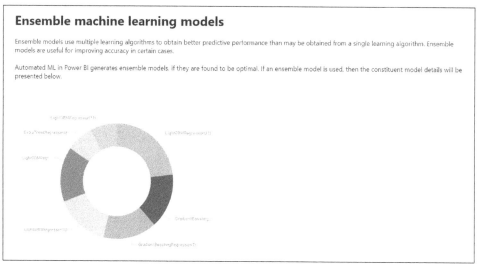

Figure 9-30. *The Ensemble model details*

This report also has an option to get feature importance or key influencing features for the model. Figure 9-31 illustrates that number of cycles and sm4 are the top features influencing the model quality.

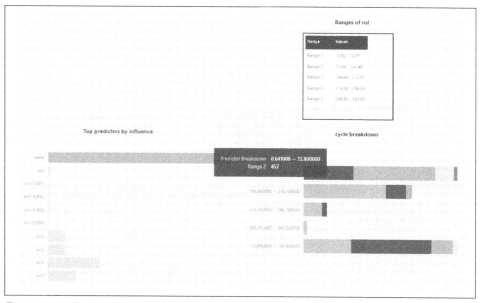

Figure 9-31. *Feature importance*

Understanding the Automated ML Training Process

The next section of the report provides details on the training process, as shown in Figure 9-32. Here, you can see the model quality across different iterations.

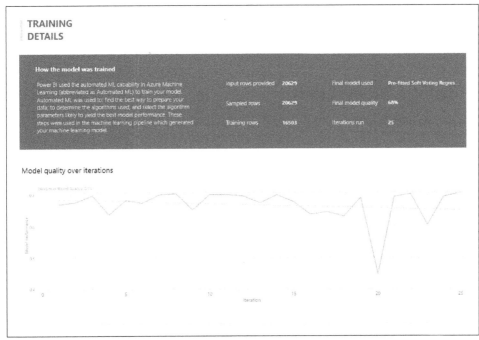

Figure 9-32. Automated ML training details

The model performance report also provides options to update the model training with new parameters and repeat the process. Figure 9-33 shows the "Edit model" option in the upper right of the screen.

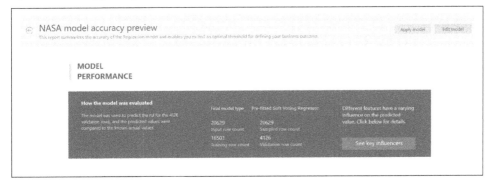

Figure 9-33. The "apply model" and "edit model" options

Model Deployment and Inferencing

When you're satisfied with the model, click the "Apply model" option from the model performance report (as shown in Figure 9-33). This takes you through a simple and intuitive flow of selecting a testing data set/entity and having column(s) added to it, which will be populated based on this trained model. As new data records come into this dataflow entity, the newly added column will be automatically populated, inferencing the model we just built and deployed.

Enabling Collaboration

So far, you have seen how automated ML is becoming available in multiple products and tools to help users of different levels of expertise train machine learning models. As enterprises begin investing more and more in machine learning and AI, a trend is emerging in which people of different roles want to collaborate to enable the end-to-end machine learning workflow. In this section, we discuss two scenarios that demonstrate this.

Azure Machine Learning to Power BI

Although automated ML in Power BI enables data analysts to easily build machine learning models, they would also like to take advantage of models built by professional data scientists from their organization. With the AI Insights feature of Power BI, it is very easy to consume any machine learning model trained using Azure Machine Learning, including those built using the Azure UI.

You saw earlier in this chapter how you can train models using the automated ML UI in Azure and deploy the trained model as a web service. With the Power BI AI Insights feature, analysts can discover and use all such deployed web services in their Power BI workloads. Let's walk through the flow.

The first step is to edit the already created dataflow entity in Power BI, as shown in Figure 9-34.

Figure 9-34. Editing a dataflow entity

Next, click "AI insights," as illustrated in Figure 9-35.

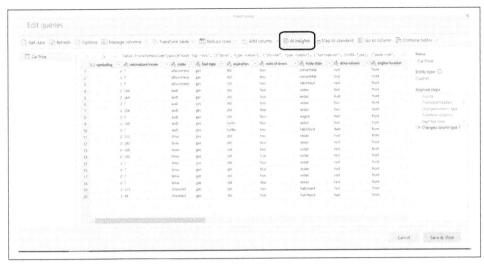

Figure 9-35. Selecting "AI insights"

This queries all Azure Machine Learning–deployed models available to use. As shown in Figure 9-36, select the relevant model for the dataflow entity that you're using and then click Apply.

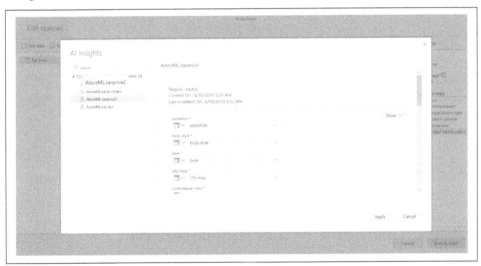

Figure 9-36. AI Insights; selecting the relevant model

This appends a new column to the entity with a prediction based on the model, as depicted in Figure 9-37.

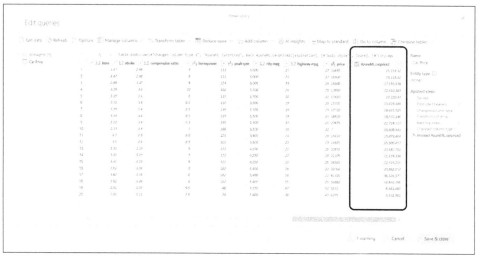

Figure 9-37. Prediction

You now understand how analysts can consume a model trained using Azure Machine Learning in Power BI. The flow from right to left in Figure 9-38 shows this collaboration scenario.

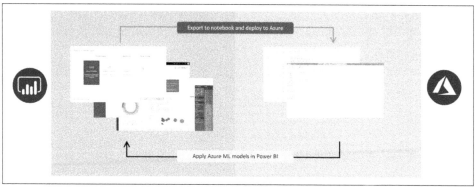

Figure 9-38. Enabling collaboration

Power BI Automated ML to Azure Machine Learning

Earlier in this chapter, you saw how analysts can use automated ML in Power BI to build machine learning models. Perhaps these analysts would like to share their models as well as training processes with professional data scientists in their organization to review, approve, or improve. This scenario could come to life if there were a way to generate Python code covering the automated ML training process that happened in Power BI. In fact, there is a way, and the flow from left to right in Figure 9-38 shows this collaboration scenario.

We expect a lot more scenarios like these to come to life in the near future to enable collaboration between different roles to make it easy to build and manage machine learning models at scale.

Conclusion

Congratulations for reaching the last chapter of the book!

In this chapter, you saw how anyone can use automated ML, regardless of their data science and Python expertise. This trend is expected to continue as automated ML continues to integrate with various products and tools that users already know and love. This demonstrates true simplification and democratization of machine learning and AI.

You began this book learning about the innovations happening in the machine learning community and on Azure. These innovations are enabling automated machine learning. You learned how Azure Machine Learning is making it possible for data scientists to manage the entire machine learning life cycle, training various types of models (e.g., classification, regression, and forecasting) using Automated Machine Learning. We also examined model interpretability and how Azure Machine Learning is providing data scientists with insights into feature importance, and more. You learned how to build container images, test the deployed model, and deploy it to various compute environments–from a REST API on Azure, to containers or edge devices, and more.

We are excited about what Automated Machine Learning will enable you to do, and we can't wait to hear about the AI solutions that you've built!

Index

About the Authors

Deepak Mukunthu is a product leader with more than 16 years of experience. With his experience in big data, analytics, and AI, Deepak has played instrumental leadership roles in helping organizations and teams become data-driven and to adopt machine learning. He brings a good mix of thought leadership, customer understanding, and innovation to design and deliver compelling products that resonate well with customers. In his current role of principal program manager of the automated ML in Azure AI platform group at Microsoft, Deepak drives product strategy and roadmap for Automated ML with the goal of accelerating AI for data scientists and democratizing AI for other personas interested in machine learning. In addition to shaping the product direction, he also plays an instrumental role in helping customers adopt Automated ML for their business-critical scenarios. Prior to joining Microsoft, Deepak worked at Trilogy where he played multiple roles—consultant, business development, program manager, engineering manager—successfully leading distributed teams across the globe and managing technical integration of acquisitions.

Parashar Shah is a senior program/product manager on the Azure AI engineering team at Microsoft, leading big data and deep learning projects to help increase adoption of AI in enterprises especially automated ML with Spark. At Microsoft and at Alcatel-Lucent/Bell Labs prior to that, his contributions increased global adoption of AI/analytics platform contributing to customers' growth in retail, manufacturing, telco, and oil and gas verticals. Parashar has an MBA from the Indian Institute of Management Bangalore and a B.E. (E.C.) from Nirma Institute of Technology, Ahmedabad. He also cofounded a carpool startup in India. He has also coauthored *Hands-On Machine Learning with Azure: Build Powerful Models with Cognitive Machine Learning and Artificial Intelligence* (Packt), published in November 2018. He has filed for five patents. He has presented at multiple Microsoft and external conferences, including Spark summit and KDD. His interests span the subjects of photography, AI, machine learning, automated ML, big data, and the internet of things (IoT).

Wee Hyong Tok is part of the AzureCAT team at Microsoft. He has extensive leadership experience leading multidisciplinary team of engineers and data scientists, working on cutting-edge AI capabilities that are infused into products and services. He is a tech visionary with a background in product management, machine learning/deep learning and working on complex engagements with customers. Over the years, he has demonstrated that his early thought leadership whitepapers on tech trends have become reality, and deeply integrated into many products. His ability to strategize, and turn strategy to execution, and hunting for customer adoption has enabled many projects that he works on to be successful. He is continuously pushing the boundaries of products for machine learning and deep learning. His team works extensively with deep learning frameworks, ranging from TensorFlow, CNTK, Keras, and PyTorch.

Wee Hyong has worn many hats in his career—developer, program/product manager, data scientist, researcher, and strategist—and his range of experience has given him unique superpowers to lead and define the strategy for high-performing data and AI innovation teams. Throughout his career, he has been a trusted advisor to the C-suite, from Fortune 500 companies to startups.

Colophon

The animal on the cover of *Practical Automated Machine Learning on Azure* is the little blue heron (*Egretta caerulea*). For most of the year these birds live in the coastal regions of the Caribbean basin, and along the equatorial coastlines of North and South America. They nest inland, in the south-central United States.

Adults average about two feet tall, with grey-blue plumage over their wings and bodies, and a deep violet head and neck. They also have a sharp, pale blue beak and long, pale yellowish-green legs.

They hunt by stalking through shallow water in freshwater, brackish, and saltwater environments, feeding on small fish, crustaceans, and insects. When they see prey in the water, they pause then advance very slowly, until when within reach; then they swiftly strike down through the water to capture their prey. Though a simple action, when striking at their prey, herons must correctly allow for how the water's surface refracts the light and shifts the image of the fish or crustacean.

When they first fledge, little blue heron chicks have white feathers, and only start to acquire their slate-blue plumage in their second year. One theory on the evolutionary advantage of this striking color change is that first-year chicks remain white when young because they can mix better with flocks of the much larger snowy egret, which both gives them protection from predators and helps them find food.

Little blue herons are at risk from habitat loss, climate changes, and water contamination. Additionally, some are legally shot each year as they hunt for fish at fish hatcheries, and human intrusion on their habitat during nesting can cause adults to abandon nests, resulting in the loss of eggs and chicks. The little blue heron currently has an IUCN Red List conservation status of being of "Least concern."

Many of the animals on O'Reilly covers are endangered; all of them are important to the world.

Color illustration by Karen Montgomery, based on a black-and-white engraving from *British Birds*. The cover fonts are Gilroy Semibold and Guardian Sans. The text font is Adobe Minion Pro; the heading font is Adobe Myriad Condensed; and the code font is Dalton Maag's Ubuntu Mono.

Lightning Source UK Ltd.
Milton Keynes UK
UKHW031008270919
350553UK00003B/21/P